AN INVITATION
TO POETRY

A NEW
FAVORITE POEM PROJECT
ANTHOLOGY

Includes a DVD Featuring Project Participants
Reading Their Favorite Poems from
Shakespeare to Szymborska

W. W. NORTON & COMPANY

An Invitation to POETRY

Edited by Robert Pinsky
and Maggie Dietz

with the editorial assistance of
Rosemarie Ellis

New York · London

Since this page cannot legibly accommodate all the copyright notices, pages 285–96
constitute an extension of the copyright page.

Manufacturing by Quebecor Fairfield
Book design by Charlotte Staub
Production manager: Julia Druskin

Library of Congress Cataloging-in-Publication Data
An invitation to poetry : a new Favorite Poem Project anthology / edited by Robert
Pinsky and Maggie Dietz with the editorial assistance of Rosemarie Ellis.— 1st ed.
p. cm.
"Includes a DVD featuring project participants."
Includes bibliographical references and index.
ISBN 0-393-05876-X (hardcover)
1. Poetry—Translations into English. 2. American poetry. 3. English poetry. I. Pinsky,
Robert. II. Dietz, Maggie. III. Ellis, Rosemarie. IV. Favorite Poem Project (U.S.)
PN6101.I56 2004
808.81—dc22

2004006210

W. W. Norton & Company, Inc., 500 Fifth Avenue, New York, N.Y. 10110
www.wwnorton.com

W. W. Norton & Company Ltd., Castle House, 75/76 Wells Street, London W1T 3QT

1 2 3 4 5 6 7 8 9 0

Contents

Acknowledgments XXI

Introduction by Robert Pinsky XXIII

CONRAD AIKEN (1889–1973) 3
from "Discordants" (1)

ANNA AKHMATOVA (1899–1966) 4
The Sentence   *DVD, Track 25*

DANTE ALIGHIERI (1265–1321) 5
The Great Canzon

YEHUDA AMICHAI (1924–2000) 7
Inside the Apple

A. R. AMMONS (1926–2001) 8
In Memoriam Mae Noblitt

JOHN ASHBERY (B. 1927) 10
A Blessing in Disguise
This Room

MARGARET ATWOOD (B. 1939) 12
It Is Dangerous to Read Newspapers

W. H. AUDEN (1907–1973) 14
Lullaby
The More Loving One

CHARLES BAUDELAIRE (1821–1867)   17
L'Invitation au Voyage

SAMUEL BECKETT (1906–1989)   19
Enueg 1
Enueg 2

JOHN BERRYMAN (1914–1972)   23
from "Eleven Addresses to Our Lord" (3, 4)

ELIZABETH BISHOP (1911–1979)   25
At the Fishhouses   *DVD, Track 26*
A Cold Spring
Some Dreams They Forgot

WILLIAM BLAKE (1757–1827)   31
The Chimney Sweeper (from *Songs of Innocence*)
The Garden of Love (from *Songs of Experience*)

LOUISE BOGAN (1897–1970)   33
The Crows
Dark Summer

EAVAN BOLAND (B. 1944)   34
The Blossom

GWENDOLYN BROOKS (1917–2000)   36
We Real Cool   *DVD, Track 8*
when you have forgotten Sunday: the love story

STERLING A. BROWN (1901–1989)   38
Strong Men

ROBERT BROWNING (1812–1889)   41
Two in the Campagna

JULIA DE BURGOS (1914–1953)   43
Ay, Ay, Ay de la Grifa Negra   *DVD, Track 12*

ROBERT BURNS (1759–1796) 45
   Is There for Honest Poverty
   John Anderson My Jo

PAUL CELAN (1920–1970) 48
   Deathfugue

WILLIAM COWPER (1731–1800) 50
   The Negro's Complaint

HART CRANE (1899–1933) 52
   Sunday Morning Apples

COUNTEE CULLEN (1903–1946) 54
   For a Poet
   Song in Spite of Myself

E. E. CUMMINGS (1894–1962) 56
   i carry your heart with me . . .

EMILY DICKINSON (1830–1886) 58
   Ample make this Bed— (829)
   The Grass so little has to do— (333)
   I'm Nobody! Who are you? (288) *DVD, Track 13*
   One need not be a Chamber—to be Haunted— (670)
   Surgeons must be very careful (108)
   To fight aloud, is very brave— (126)

JOHN DONNE (1572–1631) 62
   An Epithalamion
   The Good-Morrow

CARLOS DRUMMOND DE ANDRADE (1902–1987) 67
   The Elephant

STEPHEN DUNN (B. 1939) 70
   With No Experience in Such Matters

T. S. ELIOT (1888–1965)   72
Journey of the Magi

DAVID FERRY (B. 1924)   74
Seen through a Window

ROBERT FROST (1874–1963)   75
After Apple-Picking
Directive
An Old Man's Winter Night
"Out, Out—"   *DVD, Track 14*
The Oven Bird
The Pasture

ALLEN GINSBERG (1926–1997)   82
Transcription of Organ Music

LOUISE GLÜCK (B. 1943)   84
The School Children

JOHANN WOLFGANG VON GOETHE (1749–1842)   85
The Holy Longing   *DVD, Track 5*

THOMAS GRAY (1716–1771)   86
Ode on the Death of a Favorite Cat

THOM GUNN (B. 1929)   88
The Idea of Trust

DONALD HALL (B. 1928)   90
Woolworth's

MARK HALLIDAY (B. 1949)   91
Population

THOMAS HARDY (1840–1928)   93
Afterwards
The Man He Killed

ROBERT HASS (B. 1941)   95
Privilege of Being

ROBERT HAYDEN (1913–1980)   97
  The Night-Blooming Cereus

SEAMUS HEANEY (B. 1939)   100
  from "Clearances" (3)

ANTHONY HECHT (B. 1923)   101
  Prospects

GEORGE HERBERT (1593–1633)   102
  The Collar

ZBIGNIEW HERBERT (1924–1998)   104
  The Envoy of Mr Cogito

ROBERT HERRICK (1591–1674)   106
  Upon Julia's Clothes

GERARD MANLEY HOPKINS (1844–1889)   107
  Carrion Comfort
  God's Grandeur   DVD, Track 16
  To seem the stranger lies my lot . . .

A. E. HOUSMAN (1859–1936)   110
  When I was one-and-twenty (A Shropshire Lad 13)

LANGSTON HUGHES (1902–1967)   111
  The Dream Keeper
  Minstrel Man   DVD, Track 3
  Motto

RICHARD HUGO (1923–1982)   113
  Degrees of Gray in Philipsburg

IKKYU (1394–1481)   115
  My real dwelling

RANDALL JARRELL (1914–1965)   116
  The Islands
  The Woman at the Washington Zoo

ROBINSON JEFFERS (1887–1962) 118
The Eye

EVAN JONES (B. 1927) 119
The Song of the Banana Man   DVD, Track 18

BEN JONSON (1573–1637) 122
Inviting a Friend to Supper
Lovel's Song

DONALD JUSTICE (B. 1925) 124
Men at Forty

JOHN KEATS (1795–1821) 125
from Endymion
On a Leander Which Miss Reynolds, My Kind
    Friend, Gave Me
To Sleep

JANE KENYON (1947–1995) 128
Finding a Long Gray Hair

KENNETH KOCH (1925–2002) 129
The Boiling Water

YUSEF KOMUNYAKAA (B. 1947) 134
Facing It   DVD, Track 7

MAXINE KUMIN (B. 1925) 136
Thinking of Death and Dogfood

STANLEY KUNITZ (B. 1905) 138
Hornworm: Autumn Lamentation   DVD, Track 17
The Layers

PHILIP LARKIN (1922–1985) 141
An Arundel Tomb
The Explosion

DENISE LEVERTOV (1923–1997) 144
Caedmon

PHILIP LEVINE (B. 1928)   146
  They Feed They Lion
  What Work Is

VACHEL LINDSAY (1879–1931)   149
  The Flower-Fed Buffaloes

LI PO (701–762)   150
  Still Night Thoughts

LIU ZONGYUAN (773–819)   151
  River-Snow

HENRY WADSWORTH LONGFELLOW (1807–1882)   152
  A Psalm of Life   DVD, Track 21

RICHARD LOVELACE (1618–1657)   154
  To Althea, from Prison

ROBERT LOWELL (1917–1977)   156
  Memories of West Street and Lepke
  The Old Flame

ANTONIO MACHADO (1875–1939)   160
  Portrait

ARCHIBALD MACLEISH (1892–1982)   162
  Ars Poetica

HEATHER McHUGH (B. 1948)   163
  Language Lesson 1976

JAMES MERRILL (1926–1995)   164
  The Mad Scene

W. S. MERWIN (B. 1927)   165
  The Shore

EDNA ST. VINCENT MILLAY (1892–1950)   166
  On Hearing a Symphony of Beethoven
  Recuerdo

CZESLAW MILOSZ (B. 1911)   168
  You Who Wronged

JOHN MILTON (1608–1674)   169
  When I consider how my light is spent

GABRIELA MISTRAL (1889–1957)   170
  Piececitos   *DVD, Track 19*

MARIANNE MOORE (1887–1972)   172
  A Jellyfish
  What Are Years?

THOMAS MOORE (1779–1852)   174
  The Meeting of the Waters

HOWARD NEMEROV (1920–1991)   175
  The Snow Globe

PABLO NERUDA (1904–1973)   176
  Absence of Joaquín

LORINE NIEDECKER (1903–1970)   177
  He lived—childhood summers

FRANK O'HARA (1926–1966)   178
  The Day Lady Died
  Poem (Lana Turner has collapsed!)   *DVD, Track 6*
  Poem (And tomorrow morning at 8 o'clock
    in Springfield, Massachusetts)

GEORGE OPPEN (1908–1984)   181
  The Forms of Love
  Psalm

WILFRED OWEN (1893–1918)   183
  Dulce Et Decorum Est   *DVD, Track 20*

KENNETH PATCHEN (1911–1972)   185
  At the New Year

OCTAVIO PAZ (1914–1998)   186
Dawn
Wind and Water and Stone

FERNANDO PESSOA (1888–1935)   188
When in the widening circle of rebirth

SYLVIA PLATH (1932–1963)   189
Nick and the Candlestick   *DVD, Track 9*

EDGAR ALLAN POE (1809–1849)   191
Alone

EZRA POUND (1885–1972)   192
Erat Hora
Meditatio

ADRIENNE RICH (B. 1929)   193
The Diamond Cutters
Phantasia for Elvira Shatayev

RAINER MARIA RILKE (1875–1926)   197
Initiation
Requiem for the Death of a Boy

EDWIN ARLINGTON ROBINSON (1869–1935)   201
The Sheaves
The Unforgiven

THEODORE ROETHKE (1908–1963)   204
I Knew a Woman
In a Dark Time
The Sloth   *DVD, Track 15*

MURIEL RUKEYSER (1912–1980)   207
Effort at Speech Between Two People

SAPPHO (612 B.C.E.–?)   209
With his venom

DELMORE SCHWARTZ (1913–1966) 210
Tired and Unhappy, You Think of Houses

SIR WALTER SCOTT (1771–1832) 211
Helvellyn

ANNE SEXTON (1928–1974) 213
The Truth the Dead Know

WILLIAM SHAKESPEARE (1564–1616) 214
As an unperfect actor on the stage (*Sonnets* 23)
That time of year thou mayst in me behold
(*Sonnets* 73)
When, in disgrace with Fortune and men's eyes
(*Sonnets* 29)   **DVD, Track 11**
When forty winters shall besiege thy brow (*Sonnets* 2)

PERCY BYSSHE SHELLEY (1792–1822) 218
Love's Philosophy
Stanzas written in Dejection—December 1818, Near
Naples

EDMUND SPENSER (1552–1599) 221
Sweet is the rose, but grows upon a brere (*Amoretti* 26)

WILLIAM STAFFORD (1914–1993) 222
The Gift

GERALD STERN (B. 1925) 223
The Shirt Poem

WALLACE STEVENS (1879–1955) 227
Disillusionment of Ten O'Clock
A Rabbit as King of the Ghosts

ROBERT LOUIS STEVENSON (1850–1894) 229
My Shadow

MARK STRAND (B. 1934) 230
Keeping Things Whole

MAY SWENSON (1919–1989) 231
The Centaur

WISŁAWA SZYMBORSKA (B. 1923) 234
Notes from a Nonexistent Himalayan Expedition
DVD, Track 22

RABINDRANATH TAGORE (1861–1941) 236
from *Gitanjali* (35, 39) *DVD, Track 23*

JAMES TATE (B. 1943) 237
The Sadness of My Neighbors

ALFRED, LORD TENNYSON (1809–1892) 238
from *In Memoriam A.H.H.* (54)

ERNEST LAWRENCE THAYER (1863–1940) 239
Casey at the Bat *DVD, Track 24*

DYLAN THOMAS (1914–1953) 241
If I were tickled by the rub of love
You shall not despair

R. S. THOMAS (1913–2000) 244
The Evacuee

MARINA TSVETAEVA (1892–1941) 246
Bent with worry

PAUL VERLAINE (1844–1896) 247
Like city's rain, my heart

DEREK WALCOTT (B. 1930) 248
Streams

MARGARET WALKER (1915–1998) 250
For My People *DVD, Track 28*
Lineage

EDMUND WALLER (1606–1687) 253
Go, Lovely Rose!

ROBERT PENN WARREN (1905–1989)   254
Tell Me a Story

WALT WHITMAN (1819–1892)   255
Dirge for Two Veterans
The Runner
from *Song of Myself* (50, 52)   *DVD, Track 2*
Year That Trembled and Reel'd Beneath Me

RICHARD WILBUR (B. 1921)   259
Patriots' Day

OSCAR WILDE (1854–1900)   260
The Harlot's House

WILLIAM CARLOS WILLIAMS (1883–1963)   262
The Ivy Crown
Rain

WILLIAM WORDSWORTH (1770–1850)   268
We Are Seven
The world is too much with us; late and soon

CHARLES WRIGHT (B. 1935)   272
After Reading Tu Fu, I Go Outside to the Dwarf
   Orchard

JAMES WRIGHT (1927–1980)   273
Lying in a Hammock at William Duffy's Farm in
   Pine Island, Minnesota

THOMAS WYATT (1503–1542)   274
Whoso List To Hunt

WILLIAM BUTLER YEATS (1865–1939)   275
A Prayer for My Daughter
A Prayer for Old Age
Politics   *DVD, Track 4*

Sone no Yoshitada (late tenth century) 279
   The lower leaves of the trees   *DVD, Track 10*

Saadi Youssef (b. 1934) 280
   Attention

Zawgee (1907–1990) 281
   The Way of the Water-Hyacinth   *DVD, Track 27*

   Notes 283

   Permissions 285

   Index 297

   DVD Contents 307

Acknowledgments

Many individuals and organizations have contributed to this collection and to the success of the Favorite Poem Project since its inception in 1997.

The editors are especially grateful to the project's participants—to the thousands of people who have sent letters and e-mails, a process that continues in daily responses to the project's Web site, www.favoritepoem.org. Those participants are represented by the contributors whose comments are gathered here and in the previous anthologies *Americans' Favorite Poems* and *Poems to Read,* as well as by the readers featured in the Favorite Poem Project videos, twenty-seven of which appear on the DVD included with this book.

It would be difficult to thank sufficiently the filmmakers and crews who created the videos. Our executive producer, Juanita Anderson of Legacy Productions, guided the project with intelligence, efficiency, and imagination. We are grateful to Louis Massiah for his wise advice before, during, and after production. Four regional directors contributed talent and vision to the making of the videos: Natatcha Estébanez, Debra Farrar-Parkman, Emiko Omori, and d.b.Roderick. Their varying styles are among the collection's strengths, along with the precise, innovative editing provided by Angélica Allende Brisk. We thank Jim Lehrer, Jeffrey Brown, and Les Crystal of *The News Hour with Jim Lehrer,* which by broadcasting the videos made them available to a national audience. The National Endowment for the Arts provided major funding for video production, with additional support from the John H. and

Catherine L. Knight and the William and Flora Hewlett Foundations. We are also grateful for the vital support of Boston University, the Favorite Poem Project's administrative home.

The New England Foundation for the Arts helped us secure our first grants. The Library of Congress Center for the Book, the Academy of American Poets, and the Poetry Society of America have sponsored project events. Alice Quinn and Rachel Cohen at the Poetry Society have been valued colleagues. So has Karen Jaffe, who, while executive director of KIDSNET, was the project's partner for a distribution of materials to small and rural public libraries made possible by the Carnegie Corporation of New York.

Libraries, schools, and other organizations around the country have hosted more than a thousand Favorite Poem readings since the project launched. We thank those organizations, and the participants who read poems at those events. We owe special thanks to the teachers who've attended the Summer Poetry Institutes at Boston University and have developed valuable poetry lessons posted on the project's Web site, and to our colleagues in the Institutes, Professors Lee Indrisano and Stephan Ellenwood, of the BU School of Education. The Geraldine R. Dodge Foundation helped the project reach more teachers by sponsoring a distribution of the video segments at the Dodge Poetry Festival.

Finally, we offer deep gratitude and admiration to Rosemarie Ellis, our longtime esteemed colleague at the Favorite Poem Project, whose help with this book was invaluable.

Introduction

This anthology with its accompanying video collection demonstrates the variety of readers who find excitement and pleasure in poetry. The book also tries to fulfill the original meaning of "anthology"—from Greek, "a bouquet of flowers"—combining different selected charms, contrasts, surprises and profound dazzlements of the garden.

But to demonstrate the range of readers, each with a distinct response to a particular poem, and a range of distinguished poems, is not enough. As our title implies, we editors also hope to offer a way into poetry, through the combination of readers and poems. For someone unaccustomed to reading poetry, or who has lost the custom, an inviting way into the art or back into it. For someone devoted to poetry—maybe even for poets, teachers and scholars—a way to supplement one's sense of the art by considering examples of the infinitely various ways a poem finds its way to a reader.

What poets and teachers have to say about the art rightly has immense authority. The authority of experience, knowledge, expertise cannot be replaced. What can general readers add? Part of the answer has to do with the idea of invitation, a gesture as simple as tasting something good and then offering it to another. In the video documentaries, when Seph Rodney reads Sylvia Plath's "Nick and the Candlestick" or Stephen Conteagüero reads William Butler Yeats's "Politics" or Donna Bickel reads Stanley Kunitz's "The Hornworm," each of those poems takes place in a particular reader's voice and imagination. That visible, audible process, for the viewer, is welcoming.

We editors have tried to make a book of excellent poems, presented in the context of readers who appreciate them. The video segments created by Legacy Productions are in the same spirit, artfully dramatizing the relation between individual readers and specific poems. Executive producer Juanita Anderson led a team of producer-directors from around the country who gathered in Boston for a "production school": a few days that included technical matters like lighting, lenses, a vocabulary of shots, as well as conversations with the editors and attending a public Favorite Poem Project reading.

A central principle we gave the filmmakers was one that in a sense went against much of their training: do not illustrate the poems. If the poem is Wallace Stevens's "The Snow Man," we told them, do not show us footage of a snow man—the viewer probably knows what one looks like, and Stevens's poem describes the object to exactly the right degree. Nor were the filmmakers asked to make anything resembling a musical performance video. What we asked them to show was the relationship between each particular reader and the poem, and that is what they have succeeded in showing: the glassblower Richard Samuel amused by Frank O'Hara's "Poem"; the Cambodian immigrant Pov Chin appreciating Langston Hughes's "Minstrel Man" in relation to her family's history; Daniel McCall recalling how the memorized words of a Shakespeare sonnet have made him feel at different moments in a long life.

The reading we held when the filmmakers were in town included an economist reading a poem by Rilke and a college president reading Wallace Stevens's "The Idea of Order at Key West," along with students from the Boston Public schools reading poems by Robert Frost and Emily Dickinson, as well as Bostonians John Ulrich and John Doherty—both featured on this DVD—reading poems by Gwendolyn Brooks and Walt Whitman.

After that reading, as after other public Favorite Poem events at which a variety of people say poems they admire along with a few words about their choice, the filmmakers and I overheard members of the audience asking one another, "What would *you* choose?" This anthology sets out, among other things, to inspire the same question. Such contagions register the vitality of an art.

R.P.
Truro, MA
August 2003

AN INVITATION
TO POETRY

———————————

CONRAD AIKEN

UNITED STATES • 1889–1973

One month after my mother's death, her sister Marie, her cousin Helen, and I took the trip to Savannah that Mama had wanted for all of us. At Conrad Aiken's grave, under the Spanish moss and in view of the harbor, I recited this poem, learned by heart. I felt such a desperate need to make a fitting tribute to my mother, full of love and beauty. This was it—Aiken's gift to us.

—Doris Bucher, 55, Speech Pathologist, Atlanta, Georgia

from "Discordants"

1

Music I heard with you was more than music,
And bread I broke with you was more than bread;
Now that I am without you, all is desolate;
All that was once so beautiful is dead.

Your hands once touched this table and this silver,
And I have seen your fingers hold this glass.
These things do not remember you, belovèd,—
And yet your touch upon them will not pass.

For it was in my heart you moved among them,
And blessed them with your hands and with your eyes;
And in my heart they will remember always,—
They knew you once, O beautiful and wise.

ANNA AKHMATOVA

RUSSIA • 1899–1966

I first came across the poem in the late 1970s. It was at a time when I was beginning to come to the realization that my brother's life would never be the life that we had envisioned before he went off to Vietnam. . . . He had so many dreams, so many things he wanted to do. He was somebody you always noticed, because he was always lively and full of energy, and always there. *And the brother who came back from Vietnam was quite a contrast: my brother who left was full of life, and my brother who came back didn't have any life in him.*

—Nancy Nersessian, 51, Professor of Cognitive Science, Atlanta,
   Georgia

The Sentence

DVD, Track 25

And the stone word fell
On my still-living breast.
Never mind, I was ready.
I will manage somehow.

Today I have so much to do:
I must kill memory once and for all,
I must turn my soul to stone,
I must learn to live again—

Unless . . . Summer's ardent rustling
Is like a festival outside my window.
For a long time I've foreseen this
Brilliant day, deserted house.

Translated from the Russian by Judith Hemschemeyer

DANTE ALIGHIERI

ITALY • 1265–1321

A great love poem: simple beauty and directness—and contemporary!
—Dennis Brutus, Professor of Africana Studies, Rasburgh, Pennsylvania

The Great Canzon

I have come at last to the short
Day and the long shadow when the
Hills turn white and the grass fades. Still
Longing stays green, stuck in this hard
Stone that speaks and hears as if it was
A woman. So it was this strange
Woman stood cold as shadowed snow,
Unmoved as stone by the sweet times
When the hills turn warm and turn from
White to green and are covered with
Flowers and grass. She, when she goes
Wreathed in herbs, drives every other
Woman from my mind—shimmering
Gold with green—so lovely that love
Comes to rest in her shadow, she
Who has caught me fast between
Two hills, faster far than fused stone.
No magic gem has her power.
No herb can heal her blow. I have
Fled through the fields, over the hills,
Trying to escape from such a
Woman, but there is no wall, no
Hill, no green leaf, can ever shade
Me from her light. Time was, I saw
Her dressed all in green, so lovely
She would have made a stone love her
As I do, who love her very
Shadow. Time was, we loved once in
The grass, she loving as ever
A woman was, and the high hills
Around us. But for sure rivers

Will flow back to the hills before
This wood, full of sap and green,
Ever catch fire again from me
As lovely women do—I who
Would be glad to sleep away my
Life turned to stone, or live on grass,
If only I could be where her
Skirts would cast their shadow on me.
Now when the shadow of the hills
Is blackest, under beautiful
Green, this young woman makes it
Vanish away at last, as if
She hid a stone in the grass.

Translated from the Italian by Kenneth Rexroth

Yehuda Amichai

ISRAEL · 1924–2000

I first read "Inside the Apple" when I heard that Amichai had died. I felt numb with grief and, like a good reader of a gifted writer, drawn to reading him upon hearing the news, as if reading his words could make his death more intelligible to me. I love the sensory details of what is basically a very existentialist poem: the cool crisp apple with the "I" and the "you" somehow existing inside that quiet space; the hard lumps of pain like wax in honey. I love the simple intimacy of the poem, the biblical allusion, Amichai's sense that loss and destruction are part and parcel of human interaction.

—Susan Dickman, 39, Writer/Teacher, Evanston, Illinois

Inside the Apple

You visit me inside the apple.
Together we can hear the knife
paring around and around us, carefully,
so the peel won't tear.

You speak to me. I trust your voice
because it has lumps of hard pain in it
the way real honey
has lumps of wax from the honeycomb.

I touch your lips with my fingers:
that too is a prophetic gesture.
And your lips are red, the way a burnt field
is black.
It's all true.

You visit me inside the apple
and you'll stay with me inside the apple
until the knife finishes its work.

Translated from the Hebrew by Chana Bloch

A. R. AMMONS

UNITED STATES • 1926–2001

How many poems have been written about death, and how does one write about it without cliché? Ammons doesn't even address it directly. He backs off. This is just a place.

—Dale Wisely, 46, Clinical Psychologist, Birmingham, Alabama

In Memoriam Mae Noblitt

This is just a place:
we go around, distanced,
yearly in a star's

atmosphere, turning
daily into and out of
direct light and

slanting through the
quadrant seasons: deep
space begins at our

heels, nearly rousing
us loose: we look up
or out so high, sight's

silk almost draws us away:
this is just a place:
currents worry themselves

coiled and free in airs
and oceans: water picks
up mineral shadow and

plasm into billions of
designs, frames: trees,
grains, bacteria: but

is love a reality we
made here ourselves—
and grief—did we design

that—or do these,
like currents, whine
in and out among us merely

as we arrive and go:
this is just a place:
the reality we agree with,

that agrees with us,
outbounding this, arrives
to touch, joining with

us from far away:
our home which defines
us is elsewhere but not

so far away we have
forgotten it:
this is just a place.

JOHN ASHBERY

UNITED STATES • B. 1927

I memorized this poem five years ago and it feels as much a part of me as any organ. I recite it every day as I run the roads of Vermont.

—Katy Klutznick, 32, Editor, Burlington, Vermont

A Blessing in Disguise

Yes, they are alive and can have those colours,
But I, in my soul, am alive too.
I feel I must sing and dance, to tell
Of this in a way, that knowing you may be drawn to me.

And I sing amid despair and isolation
Of the chance to know you, to sing of me
Which are you. You see,
You hold me up to the light in a way

I should never have expected, or suspected, perhaps
Because you always tell me I am you,
And right. The great spruces loom.
I am yours to die with, to desire.

I cannot ever think of me, I desire you
For a room in which the chairs ever
Have their backs turned to the light
Inflicted on the stone and paths, the real trees

That seem to shine at me through a lattice towards you.
If the wild light of this January day is true
I pledge me to be truthful unto you
Whom I cannot ever stop remembering.

Remembering to forgive. Remember to pass beyond you into the day
On the wings of the secret you will never know.
Taking me from myself, in the path
Which the pastel girth of the day has assigned to me.

I prefer "you" in the plural, I want "you,"
You must come to me, all golden and pale
Like the dew and the air.
And then I start getting this feeling of exaltation.

I am stunned by it, and thankful for Ashbery's voice.
—Norene Cashen, 35, Publishing Account Manager/Freelance Writer,
    Farmington Hills, Michigan

This Room

The room I entered was a dream of this room.
Surely all those feet on the sofa were mine.
The oval portrait
of a dog was me at an early age.
Something shimmers, something is hushed up.

We had macaroni for lunch every day
except Sunday, when a small quail was induced
to be served to us. Why do I tell you these things?
You are not even here.

MARGARET ATWOOD

CANADA • B. 1939

When I was an infant, my father left for Vietnam, and I grew up with war as a backdrop much like Atwood's narrator. As she questions her attitudes and actions as an adult, I do the same, even more so since I am an active duty marine. She writes, "my body / is a deadly gadget, / I reach out in love, my hands are guns, / my good intentions are completely lethal." That is me—a loving, passionate soul wrapped in a trained combatant exterior.

—Barry Pawelek, 30, U.S. Marine/Student, Redondo Beach, California

It Is Dangerous to Read Newspapers

While I was building neat
castles in the sandbox,
the hasty pits were
filling with bulldozed corpses

and as I walked to the school
washed and combed, my feet
stepping on the cracks in the cement
detonated red bombs.

Now I am grownup
and literate, and I sit in my chair
as quietly as a fuse

and the jungles are flaming, the under-
brush is charged with soldiers,
the names on the difficult
maps go up in smoke.

I am the cause, I am a stockpile of chemical
toys, my body
is a deadly gadget,
I reach out in love, my hands are guns,
my good intentions are completely lethal.

Even my
passive eyes transmute
everything I look at to the pocked
black and white of a war photo,
how
can I stop myself

It is dangerous to read newspapers.

Each time I hit a key
on my electric typewriter,
speaking of peaceful trees

another village explodes.

W. H. Auden

ENGLAND • 1907–1973

When I hear the last line, it's as though an electrical storm starts inside me.
This is the ultimate poem to recite to a lover.

—Jonathan Belgard, 18, Student

Lullaby

Lay your sleeping head, my love,
Human on my faithless arm;
Time and fevers burn away
Individual beauty from
Thoughtful children, and the grave
Proves the child ephemeral:
But in my arms till break of day
Let the living creature lie,
Mortal, guilty, but to me
The entirely beautiful.

Soul and body have no bounds:
To lovers as they lie upon
Her tolerant enchanted slope
In their ordinary swoon,
Grave the vision Venus sends
Of supernatural sympathy,
Universal love and hope;
While an abstract insight wakes
Among the glaciers and the rocks
The hermit's carnal ecstasy.

Certainty, fidelity
On the stroke of midnight pass
Like vibrations of a bell
And fashionable madmen raise
Their pedantic boring cry:
Every farthing of the cost,
All the dreaded cards foretell,

Shall be paid, but from this night
Not a whisper, not a thought,
Not a kiss nor look be lost.

Beauty, midnight, vision dies:
Let the winds of dawn that blow
Softly round your dreaming head
Such a day of welcome show
Eye and knocking heart may bless,
Find our mortal world enough;
Noons of dryness find you fed
By the involuntary powers,
Nights of insult let you pass
Watched by every human love.

W. H. Auden

This poem came into my life at a time when I was feeling the deep pain of loneliness, and unrequited affection. I would take long walks at night, admiring the stars, in awe of the universe. The poem voices for me both the impossibility and the possibility of loving the darkness.

—Michaela Tauscher, 48, Secretary, Prospect Park, Pennsylvania

The More Loving One

Looking up at the stars, I know quite well
That, for all they care, I can go to hell,
But on earth indifference is the least
We have to dread from man or beast.

How should we like it were stars to burn
With a passion for us we could not return?
If equal affection cannot be,
Let the more loving one be me.

Admirer as I think I am
Of stars that do not give a damn,
I cannot, now I see them, say
I missed one terribly all day.

Were all stars to disappear or die,
I should learn to look at an empty sky
And feel its total dark sublime,
Though this might take me a little time.

W. H. Auden

CHARLES BAUDELAIRE

FRANCE • 1821–1867

I believe this poem contains the most beautiful imagery and sound ever rendered into English by way of translation. It's a union of poetic invention and the splendor of beauty.
—Cornelius Murphy, 65, Pittsburgh, Pennsylvania

L'Invitation au Voyage

My child, my sister,
              dream
How sweet all things would seem
Were we in that kind land to live together,
      And there love slow and long,
      There love and die among
Those scenes that image you, that sumptuous weather.
      Drowned suns that glimmer there
      Through cloud-disheveled air
Move me with such a mystery as appears
      Within those other skies
      Of your treacherous eyes
When I behold them shining through their tears.

There, there is nothing else but grace and measure,
Richness, quietness, and pleasure.

      Furniture that wears
      The lustre of the years
Softly would glow within our glowing chamber,
      Flowers of rarest bloom
      Proffering their perfume
Mixed with the vague fragrances of amber;
      Gold ceilings would there be,
      Mirrors deep as the sea,
The walls all in an Eastern splendor hung—
      Nothing but should address
      The soul's loneliness,
Speaking her sweet and secret native tongue.

There, there is nothing else but grace and measure,
Richness, quietness, and pleasure.

    See, sheltered from the swells
    There in the still canals
Those drowsy ships that dream of sailing forth;
    It is to satisfy
    Your least desire, they ply
Hither through all the waters of the earth.
    The sun at close of day
    Clothes the fields of hay,
Then the canals, at last the town entire
    In hyacinth and gold:
    Slowly the land is rolled
Sleepward under a sea of gentle fire.

There, there is nothing else but grace and measure,
Richness, quietness, and pleasure.

Translated from the French by Richard Wilbur

Charles Baudelaire

Samuel Beckett

IRELAND • 1906–1989

I love these poems. With the force of a few repeated words that re-sound like drums, they seal the experience of the poem into the listener's mind. They are angry, urban, bawdy, and sullen, prickling with prickled youth.

—Amy Haid, Financial Investment Professional, Columbus, Ohio

Enueg 1

Exeo in a spasm
tired of my darling's red sputum
from the Portobello Private Nursing Home
its secret things
and toil to the crest of the surge of the steep perilous bridge
and lapse down blankly under the scream of the hoarding
round the bright stiff banner of the hoarding
into a black west
throttled with clouds.

Above the mansions the algum-trees
the mountains
my skull sullenly
clot of anger
skewered aloft strangled in the cang of the wind
bites like a dog against its chastisement.

I trundle along rapidly now on my ruined feet
flush with the livid canal;
at Parnell Bridge a dying barge
carrying a cargo of nails and timber
rocks itself softly in the foaming cloister of the lock;
on the far bank a gang of down and outs would seem to be
    mending a beam.

Then for miles only wind
and the weals creeping alongside on the water
and the world opening up to the south
across a travesty of champaign to the mountains
and the stillborn evening turning a filthy green

manuring the night fungus
and the mind annulled
wrecked in wind.

I splashed past a little wearish old man,
Democritus,
scuttling along between a crutch and a stick,
his stump caught up horribly, like a claw, under his breech,
    smoking.

Then because a field on the left went up in a sudden blaze
of shouting and urgent whistling and scarlet and blue ganzies
I stopped and climbed the bank to see the game.
A child fidgeting at the gate called up:
"Would we be let in Mister?"
"Certainly" I said "you would."
But, afraid, he set off down the road.
"Well" I called after him "why wouldn't you go on in?"
"Oh" he said, knowingly,
"I was in that field before and I got put out."
So on,
derelict,
as from a bush of gorse on fire in the mountain after dark,
or, in Sumatra, the jungle hymen,
the still flagrant rafflesia.

Next:
a lamentable family of grey verminous hens,
perishing out in the sunk field,
trembling, half asleep, against the closed door of a shed,
with no means of roosting.
The great mushy toadstool,
green-black,
oozing up after me,
soaking up the tattered sky like an ink of pestilence,
in my skull the wind going fetid,
the water . . .

Next:
on the hill down from the Fox and Geese into Chapelizod
a small malevolent goat, exiled on the road,

                                                    Samuel Beckett

remotely pucking the gate of his field;
the Isolde Stores a great perturbation of sweaty heroes,
in their Sunday best,
come hastening down for a pint of nepenthe or moly or half
    and half
from watching the hurlers above in Kilmainham.

Blotches of doomed yellow in the pit of the Liffey;
the fingers of the ladders hooked over the parapet,
soliciting;
a slush of vigilant gulls in the grey spew of the sewer.

Ah the banner
the banner of meat bleeding
on the silk of the seas and the arctic flowers
that do not exist.

Enueg 2

world world world world
and the face grave
cloud against the evening

de morituris nihil nisi   •

and the face crumbling shyly
too late to darken the sky
blushing away into the evening
shuddering away like a gaffe

veronica mundi
veronica munda
give us a wipe for the love of Jesus

sweating like Judas
tired of dying
tired of policemen
feet in marmalade
perspiring profusely
heart in marmalade
smoke more fruit

the old heart the old heart
breaking outside congress
doch I assure thee
lying on O'Connell Bridge

goggling at the tulips of the evening
the green tulips
shining round the corner like an anthrax
shining on Guinness's barges

the overtone the face
too late to brighten the sky
doch doch I assure thee

John Berryman

UNITED STATES · 1914–1972

My daughter died recently, after a sixteen-year struggle with cystic fibrosis. Many were the days when the only way I continued in her caretaking was by nearly constant prayer. John Berryman's book Love and Fame *begins with the wildly entertaining adventures of a cocky, brilliant, sexual young man—ambitious, successful, and self-defeating. I, too, was self-sure and self-deprecating once. My artistic goals: acknowledgement of marvelous work, and fortune. My great passion as a mother: to be the unique anomaly who could prove doctors and their predictions wrong and save my daughter. I've managed both, in smaller ways than I imagined, and in ways unimaginable failed. Berryman's book progresses into poems of shock, dismay, disappointment, increasing despair, a breakdown, hospitalization. In the hardest dark his faith is born—the cognizance that all that's good comes not from but through him, and the awareness of his (flawed, and so human) blessings. Since my daughter's death my strength of spirit's wounded, and I've felt not able to pray. Upon reading this book I've begun to, a little. It's brought me solace and renewed strength.*

—Cynthia Lenssen, 42, Acupressure Practitioner/Teacher, San Carlos, California

from "Eleven Addresses to Our Lord"

3

Sole watchman of the flying stars, guard me
against my flicker of impulse lust: teach me
to see them as sisters & daughters. Sustain
my grand endeavours: husbandship & crafting.

Forsake me not when my wild hours come;
grant me sleep nightly, grace soften my dreams;
achieve in me patience till the thing be done,
a careful view of my achievement come.

Make me from time to time the gift of the shoulder.
When all hurt nerves whine shut away the whiskey.

Empty my heart toward Thee.
Let me pace without fear the common path of death.

Cross am I sometimes with my little daughter:
fill her eyes with tears. Forgive me, Lord.
Unite my various soul,
sole watchman of the wide & single stars.

4

If I say Thy name, art Thou there? It may be so.
Thou art not absent-minded, as I am.
I am so much so I had to give up driving.
You attend, I feel, to the matters of man.

Across the ages certain blessings swarm,
horrors accumulate, the best men fail:
Socrates, Lincoln, Christ mysterious.
Who can search Thee out?

except Isaiah & Pascal, who saw.
I dare not ask that vision, though a piece of it
at last in crisis was vouchsafèd me.
I altered then for good, to become yours.

Caretaker! take care, for we run in straits.
Daily, by night, we walk naked to storm,
some threat of wholesale loss, to ruinous fear.
Gift us with long cloaks & adrenalin.

Who haunt the avenues of Angkor Wat
recalling all that prayer, that glory dispersed,
haunt me at the corner of Fifth & Hennepin.
Shield & fresh fountain! Manifester! Even mine.

John Berryman

Elizabeth Bishop

UNITED STATES · 1911–1979

*I have one of those little palm pilots that I have the poem on, and when I
need to I sling it open and read it to whoever I can persuade to hear it. So,
I try to keep it pretty close. I've long had the feeling that life has lots of hard
edges to it. We all have suffering that comes to us in one way or another,
either from our own doing or from circumstances beyond our control, and
it's often hard to get a feel for why it's happening, or how to understand it
and stay steady and stable and keep your balance. The thing that's wonder-
ful to me about "At the Fishhouses" is the way that Bishop looks at all these
things in the world, she locates everything, including the human being—
the fisherman in the beginning—responds to it and then allows herself to
get the sensation of knowledge, which she speaks to at the very end, that
encompasses everything that she's seen and gives us . . . it's a dark sensation,
but a real, reassuring feeling that however hard things may be we can look
at it and understand it and come to terms with it.*

—Alexander Scherr, 44, Professor of Law, Athens, Georgia

At the Fishhouses   *DVD, Track 26*

Although it is a cold evening,
down by one of the fishhouses
an old man sits netting,
his net, in the gloaming almost invisible
a dark purple-brown,
and his shuttle worn and polished.
The air smells so strong of codfish
it makes one's nose run and one's eyes water.
The five fishhouses have steeply peaked roofs
and narrow, cleated gangplanks slant up
to storerooms in the gables
for the wheelbarrows to be pushed up and down on.
All is silver: the heavy surface of the sea,
swelling slowly as if considering spilling over,
is opaque, but the silver of the benches,
the lobster pots, and masts, scattered
among the wild jagged rocks,

is of an apparent translucence
like the small old buildings with an emerald moss
growing on their shoreward walls.
The big fish tubs are completely lined
with layers of beautiful herring scales
and the wheelbarrows are similarly plastered
with creamy iridescent coats of mail,
with small iridescent flies crawling on them.
Up on the little slope behind the houses,
set in the sparse bright sprinkle of grass,
is an ancient wooden capstan,
cracked, with two long bleached handles
and some melancholy stains, like dried blood,
where the ironwork has rusted.
The old man accepts a Lucky Strike.
He was a friend of my grandfather.
We talk of the decline in the population
and of codfish and herring
while he waits for a herring boat to come in.
There are sequins on his vest and on his thumb.
He has scraped the scales, the principal beauty,
from unnumbered fish with that black old knife,
the blade of which is almost worn away.

Down at the water's edge, at the place
where they haul up the boats, up the long ramp
descending into the water, thin silver
tree trunks are laid horizontally
across the gray stones, down and down
at intervals of four or five feet.

Cold dark deep and absolutely clear,
element bearable to no mortal,
to fish and to seals . . . One seal particularly
I have seen here evening after evening.
He was curious about me. He was interested in music;
like me a believer in total immersion,
so I used to sing him Baptist hymns.
I also sang "A Mighty Fortress Is Our God."

He stood up in the water and regarded me
steadily, moving his head a little.
Then he would disappear, then suddenly emerge
almost in the same spot, with a sort of shrug
as if it were against his better judgment.
Cold dark deep and absolutely clear,
the clear gray icy water . . . Back, behind us,
the dignified tall firs begin.
Bluish, associating with their shadows,
a million Christmas trees stand
waiting for Christmas. The water seems suspended
above the rounded gray and blue-gray stones.
I have seen it over and over, the same sea, the same,
slightly, indifferently swinging above the stones,
icily free above the stones,
above the stones and then the world.
If you should dip your hand in,
your wrist would ache immediately,
your bones would begin to ache and your hand would burn
as if the water were a transmutation of fire
that feeds on stones and burns with a dark gray flame.
If you tasted it, it would first taste bitter,
then briny, then surely burn your tongue.
It is like what we imagine knowledge to be:
dark, salt, clear, moving, utterly free,
drawn from the cold hard mouth
of the world, derived from the rocky breasts
forever, flowing and drawn, and since
our knowledge is historical, flowing, and flown.

Elizabeth Bishop   27

In New England the hope of spring shows itself in the first signs that it is coming: the yellow, white, purple of the crocus; the violet, that as in the poem's beginning lines, is just as soon "flawed." Spring snow, instead of spring flowers, can unexpectedly sprinkle the lawns here. I can both see and sense the hesitation of the trees, as though they can't quite read which way the weather will go. I have come to know in my daily walks many a cold spring. I know that just as each continuing line in the poem blooms, so the real world of spring will bloom as well.

—Elizabeth Farrell, 49, Homemaker/Substitute Teacher, Marion,
   Massachusetts

A Cold Spring

for Jane Dewey, Maryland

Nothing is so beautiful as spring.—HOPKINS

A cold spring:
the violet was flawed on the lawn.
For two weeks or more the trees hesitated;
the little leaves waited,
carefully indicating their characteristics.
Finally a grave green dust
settled over your big and aimless hills.
One day, in a chill white blast of sunshine,
on the side of one a calf was born.
The mother stopped lowing
and took a long time eating the after-birth,
a wretched flag,
but the calf got up promptly
and seemed inclined to feel gay.

The next day
was much warmer.
Greenish-white dogwood infiltrated the wood,
each petal burned, apparently, by a cigarette-butt;
and the blurred redbud stood
beside it, motionless, but almost more
like movement than any placeable color.
Four deer practised leaping over your fences.

The infant oak-leaves swung through the sober oak.
Song-sparrows were wound up for the summer,
and in the maple the complementary cardinal
cracked a whip, and the sleeper awoke,
stretching miles of green limbs from the south.
In his cap the lilacs whitened,
then one day they fell like snow.
Now, in the evening,
a new moon comes.
The hills grow softer. Tufts of long grass show
where each cow-flop lies.
The bull-frogs are sounding,
slack strings plucked by heavy thumbs.
Beneath the light, against your white front door,
the smallest moths, like Chinese fans,
flatten themselves, silver and silver-gilt
over pale yellow, orange, or gray.
Now, from the thick grass, the fireflies
begin to rise:
up, then down, then up again:
lit on the ascending flight,
drifting simultaneously to the same height,
—exactly like the bubbles in champagne.
—Later on they rise much higher.
And your shadowy pastures will be able to offer
these particular glowing tributes
every evening now throughout the summer.

*For the almost invisible sonnet structure and perfect rhymes; the surreal
images, the conversational tone; the dangerous dream-life in the poem; the
warning to me not to lose my dreams, to put everything down.*
—Carol Hochberg-Holker, Islamorada, Florida

Some Dreams They Forgot

The dead birds fell, but no one had seen them fly,
or could guess from where. They were black, their eyes were shut,
and no one knew what kind of birds they were. But
all held them and looked up through the new far-funneled sky.
Also, dark drops fell. Night-collected on the eaves,
or congregated on the ceilings over their beds,
they hung, mysterious drop-shapes, all night over their heads,
now rolling off their careless fingers quick as dew off leaves.
Where had they seen wood-berries perfect black as these,
shining just so in early morning? Dark-hearted decoys on
upper-bough or below-leaf. Had they thought *poison*
and left? or—remember—eaten them from the loaded trees?
What flowers shrink to seeds like these, like columbine?
But their dreams are all inscrutable by eight or nine.

Elizabeth Bishop

WILLIAM BLAKE

ENGLAND • 1757–1827

The innocent voice of the boy as he describes his terrible existence touches my heart.

—Jacqueline Bolte, 37, Librarian, Pittsburgh, Pennsylvania

The Chimney Sweeper

(from *Songs of Innocence*)

When my mother died I was very young,
And my father sold me while yet my tongue
Could scarcely cry weep weep weep weep.
So your chimneys I sweep & in soot I sleep.

There's little Tom Dacre, who cried when his head
That curl'd like a lamb's back, was shav'd, so I said,
"Hush Tom never mind it, for when your head's bare,
You know that the soot cannot spoil your white hair."

And so he was quiet, & that very night,
As Tom was a sleeping he had such a sight,
That thousands of sweepers Dick, Joe, Ned & Jack
Were all of them lock'd up in coffins of black.

And by came an Angel who had a bright key,
And he open'd the coffins & set them all free.
Then down a green plain leaping laughing they run
And wash in a river and shine in the Sun.

Then naked & white, all their bags left behind,
They rise upon clouds, and sport in the wind.
And the Angel told Tom if he'd be a good boy,
He'd have God for his father & never want joy.

And so Tom awoke and we rose in the dark
And got with our bags & our brushes to work.
Tho' the morning was cold, Tom was happy & warm,
So if all do their duty, they need not fear harm.

An adult going back to childhood haunts sees things that are hidden from a child's eyes.

—Karen Russell, 20, Secretary, Tallahassee, Florida

The Garden of Love

(from *Songs of Experience*)

I went to the Garden of Love,
And saw what I never had seen:
A Chapel was built in the midst,
Where I used to play on the green.

And the gates of this Chapel were shut,
And Thou shalt not writ over the door:
So I turn'd to the Garden of Love,
That so many sweet flowers bore,

And I saw it was filled with graves,
And tomb-stones where flowers should be:
And Priests in black gowns, were walking their rounds,
And binding with briars, my joys & desires.

Louise Bogan
UNITED STATES · 1897–1970

I read this poem when I found it in a bookstore on Commonwealth Avenue.
I was trying to find a life for myself and trying to find love. The poem
moved me, because it was bleak. It acknowledged that there will be bitter
winter burning. It still moves me.

—Joanna Woś, 50, Writer, Indianapolis, Indiana

The Crows

The woman who has grown old
And knows desire must die,
Yet turns to love again,
Hears the crows' cry.

She is a stem long hardened,
A weed that no scythe mows.
The heart's laughter will be to her
The crying of the crows,

Who slide in the air with the same voice
Over what yields not, and what yields,
Alike in spring, and when there is only bitter
Winter-burning in the fields.

I like the tender, soft shortness of it.
—Carl Adamshick, 29, Portland, Oregon

Dark Summer

Under the thunder-dark, the cicadas resound.
The storm in the sky mounts, but is not yet heard.
The shaft and the flash wait, but are not yet found.

The apples that hang and swell for the late comer,
The simple spell, the rite not for our word,
The kisses not for our mouths—light the dark summer.

EAVAN BOLAND

IRELAND • B. 1944

I am in the time of my life where my first child is leaving home and it is a time of grief and thankfulness mixed together. It is an experience like no other. This poem was, to me, the very essence of this experience from a mother's perspective. I cling to it in my moments of grief and my moments of pride and joy.

—Denise Fleming, 47, Harrison, Arkansas

The Blossom

A May morning.
Light starting in the sky.

I have come here
after a long night.
Its senses of loss.
Its unrelenting memories of happiness.

The blossom on the apple tree is still in shadow,
its petals half-white and filled with water at the core,
in which the freshness and secrecy of dawn are stored
even in the dark.

How much longer
will I see girlhood in my daughter?

In other seasons
I knew every leaf on this tree.
Now I stand here
almost without seeing them

and so lost in grief
I hardly notice what is happening
as the light increases and the blossom speaks,
and turns to me
with blonde hair and my eyebrows and says—

imagine if I stayed here,
even for the sake of your love,

what would happen to the summer?
To the fruit?

Then holds out a dawn-soaked hand to me,
whose fingers I counted at birth
years ago.

And touches mine for the last time.

And falls to earth.

GWENDOLYN BROOKS

UNITED STATES • 1917–2000

*When I was seventeen-eighteen years old, I lost six friends and neighbors,
all under twenty-five years old, to suicide. Since then I've lost about five
friends to heroine overdoses and suicide. It's like this cluster of death that
surrounds me, surrounds my neighborhood. It's kind of a desperate thing.
When I first heard "We Real Cool" in a poetry class in high school—and it
was in the middle of the cluster of suicides and all this fear that was going
on—it just made sense to me. It just really made sense: how things started
out so innocent and got so drastic so quick.*

—John Ulrich, 20, Student, South Boston, Massachusetts

We Real Cool   *DVD, Track 8*

THE POOL PLAYERS.
SEVEN AT THE GOLDEN SHOVEL.

We real cool. We
Left school. We

Lurk late. We
Strike straight. We

Sing sin. We
Thin gin. We

Jazz June. We
Die soon.

when you have forgotten Sunday: the love story

—And when you have forgotten the bright bedclothes on a
      Wednesday and a Saturday,
And most especially when you have forgotten Sunday—
When you have forgotten Sunday halves in bed,
Or me sitting on the front-room radiator in the limping afternoon
Looking off down the long street
To nowhere,
Hugged by my plain old wrapper of no-expectation
And nothing-I-have-to-do and I'm-happy-why?
And if-Monday-never-had-to-come—
When you have forgotten that, I say,
And how you swore, if somebody beeped the bell,
And how my heart played hopscotch if the telephone rang;
And how we finally went in to Sunday dinner,
That is to say, went across the front room floor to the ink-spotted
      table in the southwest corner
To Sunday dinner, which was always chicken and noodles
Or chicken and rice
And salad and rye bread and tea
And chocolate chip cookies—
I say, when you have forgotten that,
When you have forgotten my little presentiment
That the war would be over before they got to you;
And how we finally undressed and whipped out the light and
      flowed into bed,
And lay loose-limbed for a moment in the week-end
Bright bedclothes,
Then gently folded into each other—
When you have, I say, forgotten all that,
Then you may tell,
Then I may believe
You have forgotten me well.

Gwendolyn Brooks   37

STERLING A. BROWN

UNITED STATES • 1901–1989

I am moved by its strength, resolve, and resilience.
—David Barrett, 58, Manager, Columbia, Maryland

Strong Men

> *The strong men keep coming on.*—SANDBURG

They dragged you from homeland,
They chained you in coffles,
They huddled you spoon-fashion in filthy hatches,
They sold you to give a few gentlemen ease.

They broke you in like oxen,
They scourged you,
They branded you,
They made your women breeders,
They swelled your numbers with bastards. . . .
They taught you the religion they disgraced.

You sang:
> *Keep a-inchin' along*
> *Lak a po' inch worm. . . .*

You sang:
> *Bye and bye*
> *I'm gonna lay down dis heaby load. . . .*

You sang:
> *Walk togedder, chillen,*
> *Dontcha git weary. . . .*
>> The strong men keep a-comin' on
>> The strong men git stronger.

They point with pride to the roads you built for them,
They ride in comfort over the rails you laid for them.
They put hammers in your hands
And said—Drive so much before sundown.

You sang:
> *Ain't no hammah*
> *In dis lan',*
> *Strikes lak mine, bebby,*
> *Strikes lak mine.*

They cooped you in their kitchens,
They penned you in their factories,
They gave you the jobs that they were too good for,
They tried to guarantee happiness to themselves
By shunting dirt and misery to you.

You sang:
> *Me an' muh baby gonna shine, shine*
> *Me an' muh baby gonna shine.*
>> The strong men keep a-comin' on
>> The strong men git stronger. . . .

They bought off some of your leaders
You stumbled, as blind men will . . .
They coaxed you, unwontedly soft-voiced. . . .
You followed a way.
Then laughed as usual.
They heard the laugh and wondered;
Uncomfortable;
Unadmitting a deeper terror. . . .
>> The strong men keep a-comin' on
>> Gittin' stronger. . . .

What, from the slums
Where they have hemmed you,
What, from the tiny huts
They could not keep from you—
What reaches them
Making them ill at ease, fearful?
Today they shout prohibition at you
"Thou shalt not this"
"Thou shalt not that"
"Reserved for whites only"
You laugh.

One thing they cannot prohibit—
> The strong men . . . coming on
> The strong men gittin' stronger.
> Strong men. . . .
> Stronger. . . .

ROBERT BROWNING

ENGLAND · 1812–1889

*This poem takes up the subject of a love so near, but not meant to be, in a
sensitive, brilliant, and subtle way. Forever my heart will yearn.*

—Peter Elco, 52, Teacher, Absecon, New Jersey

Two in the Campagna

I wonder do you feel to-day
    As I have felt since, hand in hand,
We sat down on the grass, to stray
    In spirit better through the land,
This morn of Rome and May?

For me, I touched a thought, I know,
    Has tantalized me many times,
(Like turns of thread the spiders throw
    Mocking across our path) for rhymes
To catch at and let go.

Help me to hold it! First it left
    The yellowing fennel, run to seed
There, branching from the brickwork's cleft,
    Some old tomb's ruin: yonder weed
Took up the floating weft,

Where one small orange cup amassed
    Five beetles,—blind and green they grope
Among the honey-meal: and last,
    Everywhere on the grassy slope
I traced it. Hold it fast!

The champaign with its endless fleece
    Of feathery grasses everywhere!
Silence and passion, joy and peace,
    An everlasting wash of air—
Rome's ghost since her decease.

Such life here, through such lengths of hours,
    Such miracles performed in play,

Such primal naked forms of flowers,
        Such letting nature have her way
While heaven looks from its towers!

How say you? Let us, O my dove,
        Let us be unashamed of soul,
As earth lies bare to heaven above!
        How is it under our control
To love or not to love?

I would that you were all to me,
        You that are just so much, no more.
Nor yours nor mine, nor slave nor free!
        Where does the fault lie? What the core
O' the wound, since wound must be?

I would I could adopt your will,
        See with your eyes, and set my heart
Beating by yours, and drink my fill
        At your soul's springs,—your part my part
In life, for good and ill.

No. I yearn upward, touch you close,
        Then stand away. I kiss your cheek,
Catch your soul's warmth,—I pluck the rose
        And love it more than tongue can speak—
Then the good minute goes.

Already how am I so far
        Out of that minute? Must I go
Still like the thistle-ball, no bar,
        Onward, whenever light winds blow,
Fixed by no friendly star?

Just when I seemed about to learn!
        Where is the thread now? Off again!
The old trick! Only I discern—
        Infinite passion, and the pain
Of finite hearts that yearn.

Robert Browning

JULIA DE BURGOS

PUERTO RICO · 1914–1953

I came to Hartford in 1988, recruited by the Hartford public school system, which went to Puerto Rico looking for bilingual teachers. After that year it was a dilemma for me to decide if I'd go back to Puerto Rico or stay here for another year. I've been here for twelve years. I felt that I had a certain commitment . . . I understood the need of my children (at that point in elementary school)—they felt protected when they were with people that were familiar to them. "Ay, Ay, Ay de la Grifa Negra" is a poem that I got in contact with seven years ago and it was meaningful for me at that point in terms of my evolution here in Connecticut.

—Glaisma Pérez-Silva, 42, Bilingual Special Education Teacher,
   Hartford, Connecticut

Ay, Ay, Ay de la Grifa Negra   DVD, Track 12

Ay, ay, ay, that am kinky-haired and pure black;
kinks in my hair, Kafir in my lips;
and my flat nose Mozambiques.

Black of pure tint, I cry and laugh
the vibration of being a black statue;
a chunk of night, in which my white
teeth are lightning;
and to be a black vine
which entwines in the black
and curves the black nest
in which the raven lies.
Black chunk of black in which I sculpt myself,
ay, ay, ay, my statue is all black.

They tell me that my grandfather was the slave
for whom the master paid thirty coins.
Ay, ay, ay, that the slave was my grandfather
is my sadness, is my sadness.
If he had been the master
it would be my shame:
that in men, as in nations,

if being the slave is having no rights
being the master is having no conscience.

Ay, ay, ay, wash the sins of the white King
in forgiveness black Queen.

Ay, ay, ay, the race escapes me
and buzzes and flies toward the white race,
to sink in its clear water;
or perhaps the white will be shadowed in the black.

Ay, ay, ay, my black race flees
and with the white runs to become bronzed;
to be one for the future,
fraternity of America!

Translated from the Spanish by Jack Agüeros

ROBERT BURNS

SCOTLAND • 1759–1796

Robert Burns was a poet of humble origin. He wrote of simple yet timeless things, and of human dignity, regardless of wealth.

—Monica Bauer, Artist, Chicago, Illinois

I was born a few miles from the home of Robert Burns and learned to appreciate the universal nature of his poetry at my parents' knees. When I came to the United States as a teenager in 1949, I brought with me my love of Burns's poetry. Although I left school at fifteen (with a real dislike of the experience), the opportunity later opened for me to attend the University of Utah and I commenced a thirty-six-year adventure in the world of ideas. My introduction to higher education came shortly after I arrived from Scotland, when I was invited by Professor Jack Adamson to read the poetry of Robert Burns to his literature class. On that day, the students saw a teenage Scot read and sing his heart out, and interrupted the performance with applause and cheers on a number of occasions. When he took me home Professor Adamson suggested that I consider attending the university. When I protested that I hadn't done well enough in school in Scotland to do that, he responded "Try it—it's different here in America." I did and it was! In 1996, I retired from the University of Utah as a Professor Emeritus of Educational Studies. Thank you Professor Adamson, thank you Robert Burns, thank you America for helping me realize that indeed "A man's a man for a' that" and that I had some gold within me that was worth mining.

—Frederick S. Buchanan, 70, Retired Professor of Educational Studies,
   Salt Lake City, Utah

Is There for Honest Poverty

Is there for honest poverty
     That hings his head, an' a' that?
The coward slave, we pass him by—
     We dare be poor for a' that!
For a' that, an' a' that,
     Our toils obscure, an' a' that,
The rank is but the guinea's stamp,
     The man's the gowd for a' that.

What though on hamely fare we dine,
    Wear hoddin grey, an' a' that?
Gie fools their silks, and knaves their wine—
    A man's a man for a' that.
For a' that, an' a' that,
    Their tinsel show, an' a' that,
The honest man, tho' e'er sae poor,
    Is king o' men for a' that.

Ye see yon birkie ca'd 'a lord,'
    Wha struts, an' stares, an' a' that?
Tho' hundreds worship at his word,
    He's but a cuif for a' that.
For a' that, an' a' that,
    His ribband, star, an' a' that,
The man o' independent mind,
    He looks an' laughs at a' that.

A prince can mak a belted knight,
    A marquis, duke, an' a' that!
But an honest man's aboon his might—
    Guid faith, he mauna fa' that!
For a' that, an' a' that,
    Their dignities, an' a' that,
The pith o' sense an' pride o' worth
    Are higher rank than a' that.

Then let us pray that come it may
    (As come it will for a' that)
That Sense and Worth o'er a' the earth
    Shall bear the gree an' a' that!
For a' that, an' a' that,
    It's comin yet for a' that,
That man to man the world o'er
    Shall brithers be for a' that.

John Anderson My Jo

John Anderson my jo, John,
     When we were first acquent,
Your locks were like the raven,
     Your bonie brow was brent;
But now your brow is beld, John,
     Your locks are like the snaw,
But blessings on your frosty pow,
     John Anderson my jo!

John Anderson my jo, John,
     We clamb the hill thegither,
And monie a cantie day, John,
     We've had wi' ane anither;
Now we maun totter down, John,
     And hand in hand we'll go,
And sleep thegither at the foot,
     John Anderson my jo!

PAUL CELAN

ROMANIA · 1920–1970

It seems to apply the lotion of equal vision to one of the great horrors of our time and to try to see it as perhaps God saw it.

—Sarah Chace, 41, Academic Administrator, Cambridge, Massachusetts

Deathfugue

Black milk of daybreak we drink it at evening
we drink it at midday and morning we drink it at night
we drink and we drink
we shovel a grave in the air where you won't lie too cramped
A man lives in the house he plays with his vipers he writes
he writes when it grows dark to Deutschland your golden hair
    Margareta
he writes it and steps out of doors and the stars are all sparkling he
    whistles his hounds to stay close
he whistles his Jews into rows has them shovel a grave in the
    ground
he commands us play up for the dance

Black milk of daybreak we drink you at night
we drink you at morning and midday we drink you at evening
we drink and we drink
A man lives in the house he plays with his vipers he writes
he writes when it grows dark to Deutschland your golden hair
    Margareta
Your ashen hair Shulamith we shovel a grave in the air where you
    won't lie too cramped

He shouts dig this earth deeper you lot there you others sing up
    and play
he grabs for the rod in his belt he swings it his eyes are so blue
stick your spades deeper you lot there you others play on for the
    dancing

Black milk of daybreak we drink you at night
we drink you at midday and morning we drink you at evening
we drink and we drink

a man lives in the house your goldenes Haar Margareta
your aschenes Haar Shulamith he plays with his vipers

He shouts play death more sweetly this Death is a master from
    Deutschland
he shouts scrape your strings darker you'll rise up as smoke to the
    sky
you'll then have a grave in the clouds where you won't lie too
    cramped

Black milk of daybreak we drink you at night
we drink you at midday Death is a master aus Deutschland
we drink you at evening and morning we drink and we drink
this Death is ein Meister aus Deutschland his eye it is blue
he shoots you with shot made of lead shoots you level and true
a man lives in the house your goldenes Haar Margarete
he looses his hounds on us grants us a grave in the air
he plays with his vipers and daydreams der Tod ist ein Meister aus
    Deutschland

dein goldenes Haar Margarete
dein aschenes Haar Sulamith

Translated from the German by John Felstiner

WILLIAM COWPER

ENGLAND · 1731–1800

William Cowper wrote with feeling, but more so with understanding. Though written years ago, this poem pertains to the "human aspect," and is still appropriate today, as the many races learn to live together.

—Joyce Pierandrea, 56, Retired, Worcester, Massachusetts

The Negro's Complaint

Forced from home, and all its pleasures,
     Afric's coast I left forlorn;
To increase a stranger's treasures,
     O'er the raging billows borne,
Men from England bought and sold me,
     Paid my price in paltry gold;
But, though theirs they have enrolled me,
     Minds are never to be sold.

Still in thought as free as ever,
     What are England's rights, I ask,
Me from my delights to sever,
     Me to torture, me to task?
Fleecy locks, and black complexion
     Cannot forfeit nature's claim;
Skins may differ, but affection
     Dwells in white and black the same.

Why did all-creating Nature
     Make the plant for which we toil?
Sighs must fan it, tears must water,
     Sweat of ours must dress the soil.
Think, ye masters, iron-hearted,
     Lolling at your jovial boards;
Think how many backs have smarted
     For the sweets your cane affords.

Is there, as ye sometimes tell us,
     Is there one who reigns on high?
Has he bid you buy and sell us,

Speaking from his throne the sky?
Ask him, if your knotted scourges,
  Matches, blood-extorting screws,
Are the means which duty urges
  Agents of his will to use?

Hark! he answers—Wild tornadoes,
  Strewing yonder sea with wrecks;
Wasting towns, plantations, meadows,
  Are the voice with which he speaks.
He, foreseeing what vexations
  Afric's sons should undergo,
Fixed their tyrants' habitations
  Where his whirlwinds answer—No.

By our blood in Afric wasted,
  Ere our necks received the chain;
By the mis'ries we have tasted,
  Crossing in your barks the main;
By our suff'rings since ye brought us
  To the man-degrading mart;
All sustained by patience, taught us
  Only by a broken heart:

Deem our nation brutes no longer
  Till some reason ye shall find
Worthier of regard and stronger
  Than the colour of our kind.
Slaves of gold, whose sordid dealings
  Tarnish all your boasted pow'rs,
Prove that you have human feelings,
  Ere you proudly question ours!

William Cowper

HART CRANE

UNITED STATES • 1899–1933

The Brandywine Valley that is mentioned in the poem is not the famous one of the Wyeths, but part of the watershed of the Cuyahoga River in Ohio. It has a good waterfall and it is now part of the Cuyahoga Valley National Recreation Area. The William Sommer to whom the poem is addressed is Cleveland's great early modernist painter (active here from 1900 to 1948). He knew cubism, he knew regionalism, and he knew the light of the valley in which he made his home. The home where I lived from grades one to twelve, built by my father, overlooked a nearby valley, part of the same watershed. So this poem mixes much of what has been important in my life and stirs the ingredients into a nice stew. And then, of course: the seasonable madness, the apples!

—William Busta, 50, Art Curator, Cleveland Heights, Ohio

Sunday Morning Apples

To William Sommer

The leaves will fall again sometime and fill
The fleece of nature with those purposes
That are your rich and faithful strength of line.

But now there are challenges to spring
In that ripe nude with head
                    reared
Into a realm of swords, her purple shadow
Bursting on the winter of the world
From whiteness that cries defiance to the snow.

A boy runs with a dog before the sun, straddling
Spontaneities that form their independent orbits,
Their own perennials of light
In the valley where you live
                    (called Brandywine).

I have seen the apples there that toss you secrets,—
Beloved apples of seasonable madness

That feed your inquiries with aerial wine.
Put them again beside a pitcher with a knife,
And poise them full and ready for explosion—
The apples, Bill, the apples!

COUNTEE CULLEN

UNITED STATES • 1903–1946

*It remains for me a song sustaining hope in the face of dreams unrealized,
a sort of acceptance of a thing not to be.*

—Freddie Robinson, Paterson, New Jersey

For a Poet

To John Gaston Edgar

I have wrapped my dreams in a silken cloth,
And laid them away in a box of gold;
Where long will cling the lips of the moth,
I have wrapped my dreams in a silken cloth;
I hide no hate; I am not even wroth
Who found earth's breath so keen and cold;
I have wrapped my dreams in a silken cloth,
And laid them away in a box of gold.

It talks about how people should love—not by putting their whole heart in a relationship, since there are chances the heart could be broken. Now any-time I look for a girl, I will give her some of my love, but at the same time, keep my distance.

—Carlton Francis, Student, Brooklyn, New York

Song in Spite of Myself

Never love with all your heart,
　　It only ends in aching;
And bit by bit to the smallest part
　　That organ will be breaking.

Never love with all your mind,
　　It only ends in fretting;
In musing on sweet joys behind,
　　Too poignant for forgetting.

Never love with all your soul,
　　For such there is no ending,
Though a mind that frets may find control,
　　And a shattered heart find mending.

Give but a grain of the heart's rich seed,
　　Confine some under cover,
And when love goes, bid him God-speed.
　　And find another lover.

E. E. CUMMINGS

UNITED STATES · 1894–1962

When I was in boarding school and in college, I loved this poem and I still had that idealized notion of finding someone to read it to, with all the passion and fierce love that one's first love affair brings. One soon learns it is very hard work to seek and find love, to make love fit into each day, and into one's career, while trying to keep abreast of the car and mortgage payments, and the groceries in the refrigerator. The love affairs began and ended. I matured. In my thirties, my career succeeded and I married. In my forties, I conceived a child, and under circumstances wholly unimagined, found someone to read the poem to: in August 2001, I delivered my first child, Ella, a girl. At birth she had suffered a cranial hemorrhage that caused her no pain and left her nonresponsive. Her body was kept on life support for six days to fulfill the hospital's legal requirement to pronounce her brain dead and to establish the viability of her organs for transplant. Days later autopsy results revealed that a brain tumor had begun early in her fetal development and had spread to the brain stem and spinal cord. On August 21, 2001, my newborn daughter Ella gave away her heart. It now belongs to an infant boy in Michigan. In those days with my daughter, this poem stuck in my mind, and took on a most prescient, personal tone. I told it to her with great passion and with fierce love, as she lay in the incubator, just minutes before she entered surgery to offer her heart.

—Heidi Hughes, 43, Consultant, Trenton, New Jersey

i carry your heart with me . . .

i carry your heart with me(i carry it in
my heart)i am never without it(anywhere
i go you go,my dear;and whatever is done
by only me is your doing,my darling)
                              i fear
no fate(for you are my fate,my sweet)i want
no world(for beautiful you are my world,my true)
and it's you are whatever a moon has always meant
and whatever a sun will always sing is you

E. E. Cummings

here is the deepest secret nobody knows
(here is the root of the root and the bud of the bud
and the sky of the sky of a tree called life;which grows
higher than soul can hope or mind can hide)
and this is the wonder that's keeping the stars apart

i carry your heart(i carry it in my heart)

EMILY DICKINSON

UNITED STATES · 1830–1886

Peace, sleep, rest implicit in each word. Sanctification layered beneath.
Beautiful yet simple—yet textured—levels.
—Robert Young, 46, Bartender, Terre Haute, Indiana

Ample make this Bed— (829)

Ample make this Bed—
Make this Bed with Awe—
In it wait till Judgment break
Excellent and Fair.

Be its Mattress straight—
Be its Pillow round—
Let no Sunrise' yellow noise
Interrupt this Ground—

I come from a family of seven children. In the evenings, as a child, I would
participate in family readings in our living room before bedtime. I remem-
ber many poems we read aloud together quite well, including portions of
The Iliad *and* The Odyssey *read by my brother, poems by Frost and*
Sandburg, Longfellow, Nash and many others. My favorite memory is of
this wonderful poem read aloud by my mother. I can still hear her voice so
clearly in my imagination as I recite it to myself from memory. And the
poem reminds me of my mother, too. It is about humility.
—Martin Dickinson, 54, Nonprofit Development Director, Washington,
    District of Columbia

The Grass so little has to do— (333)

The Grass so little has to do—
A Sphere of simple Green—
With only Butterflies to brood
And Bees to entertain—

And stir all day to pretty Tunes
The Breezes fetch along—
And hold the Sunshine in its lap
And bow to everything—

And thread the Dews, all night, like Pearls—
And make itself so fine
A Duchess were too common
For such a noticing—

And even when it dies—to pass
In Odors so divine—
Like Lowly spices, lain to sleep—
Or Spikenards, perishing—

And then, in Sovereign Barns to dwell—
And dream the Days away,
The Grass so little has to do
I wish I were a Hay—

*I discovered this poem in seventh grade when one of my English teachers
showed it to me. And then eighth grade came and ninth grade, and every
year as life gets busier the poem keeps on coming back to me . . . so much
better every time, that I think in time it discovered me.*

—Yina Liang, 16, Student, Atlanta, Georgia

I'm Nobody! Who are you? (288)   *DVD, Track 13*

I'm Nobody! Who are you?
Are you—Nobody—Too?
Then there's a pair of us!
Don't tell! they'd advertise—you know!

How dreary—to be—Somebody!
How public—like a Frog—
To tell one's name—the livelong June—
To an admiring Bog!

Emily Dickinson knew that the things we need to fear the most are not outside of us, but within. No one says it better than she does!
—Wanda Richardson, 48, Ultrasonographer, Eagle Springs, North
  Carolina

One need not be a Chamber—to be Haunted— (670)

One need not be a Chamber—to be Haunted—
One need not be a House—
The Brain has Corridors—surpassing
Material Place—

Far safer, of a Midnight Meeting
External Ghost
Than its interior Confronting—
That Cooler Host.

Far safer, through an Abbey gallop,
The Stone a'chase—
Than Unarmed, one's a'self encounter—
In lonesome Place—

Ourself behind ourself, concealed—
Should startle most—
Assassin hid in our Apartment
Be Horror's least.

The Body—borrows a Revolver—
He bolts the Door—
O'erlooking a superior spectre—
Or More—

Surgeons must be very careful (108)

Surgeons must be very careful
When they take the knife!
Underneath their fine incisions
Stirs the Culprit—*Life!*

To fight aloud, is very brave— (126)

To fight aloud, is very brave—
But *gallanter,* I know
Who charge within the bosom
The Cavalry of Woe—

Who win, and nations do not see—
Who fall—and none observe—
Whose dying eyes, no Country
Regards with patriot love—

We trust, in plumed procession
For such, the Angels go—
Rank after Rank, with even feet—
And Uniforms of Snow.

Emily Dickinson

JOHN DONNE

ENGLAND · 1572–1631

I loved this poem from the moment I read it first, in college. I didn't know who I was reading it for until I met the man I married. Our first date extended into Valentine's Day. A bit more than one year later, we read Donne's poem at our wedding.

—Yvonne Coats, 43, Science Fiction Writer, Albuquerque, New Mexico

An Epithalamion, Or Marriage Song, on the Lady Elizabeth and Count Palatine Being Married on St. Valentine's Day

Hail Bishop Valentine, whose day this is,
    All the air is thy diocese,
    And all the chirping choristers
And other birds are thy parishioners;
    Thou marriest every year
The lyric lark, and the grave whispering dove,
The sparrow that neglects his life for love,
The household bird with the red stomacher;
    Thou mak'st the blackbird speed as soon,
As doth the goldfinch, or the halcyon;
The husband cock looks out, and straight is sped,
And meets his wife, which brings her feather-bed.
This day more cheerfully than ever shine,
This day, which might inflame thyself, old Valentine.

Till now, thou warmed'st with multiplying loves
    Two larks, two sparrows, or two doves.
    All that is nothing unto this,
For thou this day couplest two phoenixes;
    Thou mak'st a taper see
What the sun never saw; and what the Ark
(Which was of fowls and beasts the cage and park,)
Did not contain, one bed contains, through thee—
    Two phoenixes, whose joinèd breasts
Are unto one another mutual nests,
Where motion kindles such fires as shall give

Young phoenixes, and yet the old shall live;
Whose love and courage never shall decline,
But make the whole year through thy day, O Valentine.

Up then fair phoenix bride, frustrate the sun,
  Thyself from thine affection
  Tak'st warmth enough, and from thine eye
All lesser birds will take their jollity.
  Up, up, fair bride, and call
Thy stars from out their several boxes, take
Thy rubies, pearls, and diamonds forth, and make
Thyself a constellation of them all,
  And by their blazing signify,
That a great princess falls, but doth not die;
Be thou a new star, that to us portends
Ends of much wonder; and be thou those ends.
Since thou dost this day in new glory shine,
May all men date records from this thy Valentine.

Come forth, come forth, and as one glorious flame,
  Meeting another, grows the same,
  So meet thy Frederick, and so
To an inseparable union grow.
  Since separation
Falls not on such things as are infinite,
Nor things which are but one, can disunite,
You're twice inseparable, great, and one;
  Go, then, to where the bishop stays,
To make you one, his way, which divers ways
Must be effected; and when all is past,
And that you're one, by hearts and hands made fast,
You two have one way left, yourselves to entwine,
Besides this bishop's knot, or Bishop Valentine.

But oh, what ails the sun, that here he stays
  Longer today, than other days?
  Stays he new light from these to get,
And finding here such store, is loath to set?
  And why do you two walk,
So slowly-paced in this procession?

Is all your care but to be looked upon,
And be to others spectacle and talk?
    The feast, with gluttonous delays,
Is eaten, and too long their meat they praise,
The masquers come late, and I think will stay,
Like fairies, till the cock crow them away.
Alas, did not antiquity assign
A night, as well as day, to thee, O Valentine?

They did, and night is come; and yet we see
    Formalities retarding thee.
    What mean these ladies, which (as though
They were to take a clock in pieces) go
    So nicely about the bride?
A bride, before a good-night could be said,
Should vanish from her clothes into her bed,
As souls from bodies steal, and are not spied.
    But now she's laid; what though she be?
Yet there are more delays, for, where is he?
He comes, and passes through sphere after sphere:
First her sheets, then her arms, then anywhere.
Let not this day, then, but this night be thine;
Thy day was but the eve to this, O Valentine.

Here lies a she-sun, and a he-moon here;
    She gives the best light to his sphere;
    Or each is both, and all, and so
They unto one another nothing owe;
    And yet they do, but are
So just and rich in that coin which they pay,
That neither would nor needs forbear nor stay;
Neither desires to be spared, nor to spare;
    They quickly pay their debt, and then
Take no acquittances, but pay again;
They pay, they give, they lend, and so let fall
No such occasion to be liberal.
More truth, more courage in these two do shine,
Than all thy turtles have, and sparrows, Valentine.

John Donne

And by this act of these two phoenixes
    Nature again restorèd is,
    For since these two are two no more,
There's but one phoenix still, as was before.
    Rest now at last, and we
As satyrs watch the sun's uprise, will stay
Waiting when your eyes opened let out day,
Only desired because your face we see;
    Others near you shall whispering speak,
And wagers lay, at which side day will break,
And win by observing, then, whose hand it is
That opens first a curtain, hers or his;
This will be tried tomorrow after nine,
Till which hour we thy day enlarge, O Valentine.

The Good-Morrow

I wonder, by my troth, what thou and I
Did till we loved? Were we not weaned till then,
But sucked on country pleasures childishly?
Or snorted we in the seven sleepers' den?

'Twas so; but this, all pleasures fancies be.
If ever any beauty I did see
Which I desired, and got, 'twas but a dream of thee.

And now good morrow to our waking souls,
Which watch not one another out of fear;
For love all love of other sights controls,
And makes one little room an everywhere.
Let sea-discoverers to new worlds have gone,
Let maps to other, worlds on worlds have shown,
Let us possess one world: each hath one, and is one.

My face in thine eye, thine in mine appears,
And true plain hearts do in the faces rest.
Where can we find two better hemispheres,
Without sharp North, without declining West?
Whatever dies was not mixed equally;
If our two loves be one, or thou and I
Love so alike that none do slacken, none can die.

CARLOS DRUMMOND DE ANDRADE

BRAZIL • 1902–1987

For better or worse: I am the elephant. We are the elephant.
—Katheryn Doran, 45, Philosophy Professor, Clinton, New York

The Elephant

I make an elephant
from the little
I have. Wood
from old furniture
holds him up,
and I fill him
with cotton, silk,
and sweetness.
Glue keeps his heavy
ears in place.
His rolled-up trunk
is the happiest part
of his architecture.
But there are also
his tusks made
of that rare material
I cannot fake.
What a white fortune
to be rolling around
in the dust of the circus
without being stolen or lost!
And finally there are
the eyes where the most
fluid and permanent
part of the elephant
stays, free of all fraud.

Here's my poor elephant
ready to leave
to find friends
in a jaded world
that no longer believes

Carlos Drummond de Andrade

in animals and doesn't
trust things.
Here he is: an imposing
and fragile hulk,
who shakes his head
and moves slowly,
his hide stitched
with cloth flowers
and clouds, allusions
to a more poetic world
where love reassembles
the natural forms.

My elephant goes
down a crowded street,
but nobody looks
not even to laugh
at his tail that threatens
to leave him.
He is all grace, except
his legs don't help
and his swollen belly
is about to collapse
at the slightest touch.
He expresses
with elegance
his minimal life
and no one in town
is willing to take
to himself
from that tender body
the fugitive image,
the clumsy walk,
hungry and touching,
but hungry for pitiful
people and situations,
for moonlit encounters
in the deepest ocean,
under the roots of trees
or in the bosom of shells,

Carlos Drummond de Andrade

for lights that do not blind
yet shine through
the thickest trunks.
That walk which goes
without crushing plants
on the battlefield,
searching for places,
secrets, stories
untold in any book,
whose style only the wind,
the leaves, the ant
recognize, but men
ignore since they dare
show themselves only
under a veiled peace
and to closed eyes.

And now late at night
my elephant returns,
but returns tired out,
his shaky legs
break down in the dust.
He didn't find
what he wanted,
what we wanted,
I and my elephant,
in whom I love
to disguise myself.
Tired of searching,
his huge machinery
collapses like paper.
The paste gives way
and all his contents,
forgiveness, sweetness,
feathers, cotton,
burst out on the rug,
like a myth torn apart.
Tomorrow I begin again.

Translated from the Portuguese by Mark Strand

Carlos Drummond de Andrade

STEPHEN DUNN

UNITED STATES • B. 1939

*My father died in July of 1984, at the age of eighty-three, in a hospital
room in Encinitas, California. As he lay in his hospital bed, terminally
comatose, I had a singular moment with him, two days before he died, that
shook me. My father and my mother had come up from Florida for the
summer to stay with me. We all, my brother and sister, too, had tickets to
the Olympic Games in Los Angeles. My father had suffered a massive brain
hemorrhage and was rendered brain dead. After he lay this way for three
days, the family agreed among themselves, and with the doctor's concur-
rence, that keeping my father on life support was just using artificial means
in a hopeless situation. The ordeal of suspended grieving was wearing down
the whole family, especially my not-too-healthy mother. We decided to "pull
the plug" on Dad's life. It was done. The solution that was dripping into
my father's vein was changed from food to saline. It was with terrible mixed
emotions that we then waited for his stubbornly strong heart to stop. A day
or two later, and still no change in his condition (what a heart he had!), I
came into his hospital room to be with him. I sat there looking at my father
as the monitor registered his heartbeat, as the lung machine pumped up
and down—just to be there. I spoke to my father as he lay there, and said
the only thing I could think of: "Come on Pop, come out of this coma. You
know we all came here to go the Olympics. The whole family is waiting." I
don't know what I was thinking, other than trying to relieve my feelings of
guilt and helplessness. But because of what happened next, my words and
that moment were seared into my memory forever. I swear: the heart mon-
itor, which for days had kept up a never-changing pattern and rhythm,
showed a quickening. He had heard me! Feelings of panic, and shame, and
fear of the unknown knotted my gut. The pain that lingers still from that
moment doesn't come from any sense of guilt that he ever had any chance of
coming alive, but from not having thought of my Dad at that moment,
but only of myself. I was speaking the conventional encouragements one
does with a convalescent, to make myself feel noble and relieved for the
effort. I had no idea he was eavesdropping. Why didn't I say: "It's OK Pop,
you can let go. You can relax. Your work is done. The whole family is in
good shape"? Within a couple of days, his heart finally stopped. As I said,*

the memory of it all, and the accompanying pain, lingers. Some years later
I read Stephen Dunn's poem.

—Leonard Oberman, 72, Retired, Carlsbad, California

With No Experience in Such Matters

To hold a damaged sparrow
under water until you feel it die
is to know a small something
about the mind; how, for example,
it blames the cat for the original crime,
how it wants praise for its better side.

And yet it's as human
as pulling the plug on your Dad
whose world has turned
to feces and fog, human as . . .
well, let's admit, it's a mild thing
as human things go.

But I felt the one good wing
flutter in my palm—
the smallest protest, if that's what it was,
I ever felt or heard.
Reminded me how my eyelid has twitched,
the need to account for it.
Hard to believe no one notices.

T. S. ELIOT

UNITED STATES · 1888–1965

I find it chilling. My high school English teacher read it aloud to us one spring day, and the words of the poem have remained with me, in his voice, ever since.

—Kim Colwell, Palo Alto, California

Journey of the Magi

"A cold coming we had of it,
Just the worst time of the year
For a journey, and such a long journey:
The ways deep and the weather sharp,
The very dead of winter."
And the camels galled, sore-footed, refractory,
Lying down in the melting snow.
There were times we regretted
The summer palaces on slopes, the terraces,
And the silken girls bringing sherbet.
Then the camel men cursing and grumbling
And running away, and wanting their liquor and women,
And the night-fires going out, and the lack of shelters,
And the cities hostile and the towns unfriendly
And the villages dirty and charging high prices:
A hard time we had of it.
At the end we preferred to travel all night,
Sleeping in snatches,
With the voices singing in our ears, saying
That this was all folly.

Then at dawn we came down to a temperate valley,
Wet, below the snow line, smelling of vegetation;
With a running stream and a water-mill beating the darkness,
And three trees on the low sky,
And an old white horse galloped away in the meadow.
Then we came to a tavern with vine-leaves over the lintel,
Six hands at an open door dicing for pieces of silver,
And feet kicking the empty wine-skins.

But there was no information, and so we continued
And arrived at evening, not a moment too soon
Finding the place; it was (you may say) satisfactory.

   All this was a long time ago, I remember,
And I would do it again, but set down
This set down
This: were we led all that way for
Birth or Death? There was a Birth, certainly,
We had evidence and no doubt. I had seen birth and death,
But had thought they were different; this Birth was
Hard and bitter agony for us, like Death, our death.
We returned to our places, these Kingdoms,
But no longer at ease here, in the old dispensation,
With an alien people clutching their gods.
I should be glad of another death.

T. S. Eliot   73

DAVID FERRY

UNITED STATES · B. 1924

I read it and feel like I have been passed a slip of paper with a beautiful secret written on it, and I have been part of the world the poet shares—and this is good, because often I feel isolation in it. And the music of his words: somehow he manages to struggle, and to be stark or imaginative, and still sound like the kind of soft music we play as medicine for people who are hurting.

—Nicole Long, 32, Hospice Volunteer Coordinator, Salisbury, Maryland

Seen through a Window

A man and a woman are sitting at a table.
It is supper time. The air is green. The walls
Are white in the green air, as rocks under water
Retain their own true color, though washed in green.
I do not know either the man or the woman,
Nor do I know whatever they know of each other.
Though washed in my eye they keep their own true color.

The man is all his own hunched strength, the body's
Self and strength, that bears, like weariness,
Itself upon itself, as a stone's weight
Bears heavily on itself to be itself.
Heavy the strength that bears the body down.
And the way he feeds is like a dreamless sleep;
The dreaming of a stone is how he feeds.

The woman's arms are plump, mottled a little
The flesh, like standing milk, and on one arm
A blue bruise, got in some household labor or other,
Flowering in the white. Her staring eye,
Like some bird's cry called from some deepest wood,
Says nothing of what it is but what it is.
Such silence is the bird's cry of a stone.

ROBERT FROST

UNITED STATES • 1874–1963

My grandfather recently passed away and I take comfort in Frost's vision of a previous America. The texture of the trees, the fragrance of the apples, "the pressure of the ladder-round" on the narrator's feet—all of these contribute to the sense that life is beautiful and magical and must be snatched up. But there's also a cycle to these things not to be overcome—and at some point you reach your fill even of apples.

—Kristin Roper, 19, Student, Alpine, New Jersey

After Apple-Picking

My long two-pointed ladder's sticking through a tree
Toward heaven still,
And there's a barrel that I didn't fill
Beside it, and there may be two or three
Apples I didn't pick upon some bough.
But I am done with apple-picking now.
Essence of winter sleep is on the night,
The scent of apples: I am drowsing off.
I cannot rub the strangeness from my sight
I got from looking through a pane of glass
I skimmed this morning from the drinking trough
And held against the world of hoary grass.
It melted, and I let it fall and break.
But I was well
Upon my way to sleep before it fell,
And I could tell
What form my dreaming was about to take.
Magnified apples appear and disappear,
Stem end and blossom end,
And every fleck of russet showing clear.
My instep arch not only keeps the ache,
It keeps the pressure of a ladder-round.
I feel the ladder sway as the boughs bend.
And I keep hearing from the cellar bin
The rumbling sound
Of load on load of apples coming in.

For I have had too much
Of apple-picking: I am overtired
Of the great harvest I myself desired.
There were ten thousand thousand fruit to touch,
Cherish in hand, lift down, and not let fall.
For all
That struck the earth,
No matter if not bruised or spiked with stubble,
Went surely to the cider-apple heap
As of no worth.
One can see what will trouble
This sleep of mine, whatever sleep it is.
Were he not gone,
The woodchuck could say whether it's like his
Long sleep, as I describe its coming on,
Or just some human sleep.

I find myself returning to this poem when my situation is uncertain or
chaotic or I am experiencing loss. Frost tells us that taking the spiritual
journey is risky, nothing is certain, tranquillity is not a guarantee, and we
have to give up some things. The promise of the poem seems to be that when
we are lost enough to find ourselves and pull in the ladder behind us, the
loss creates a vacuum into which will come something new and better.
—Susan Patton, 51, Healthcare Administrator, Austin, Texas

Directive

Back out of all this now too much for us,
Back in a time made simple by the loss
Of detail, burned, dissolved, and broken off
Like graveyard marble sculpture in the weather,
There is a house that is no more a house
Upon a farm that is no more a farm
And in a town that is no more a town.
The road there, if you'll let a guide direct you
Who only has at heart your getting lost,
May seem as if it should have been a quarry—

Great monolithic knees the former town
Long since gave up pretense of keeping covered.
And there's a story in a book about it:
Besides the wear of iron wagon wheels
The ledges show lines ruled southeast-northwest,
The chisel work of an enormous Glacier
That braced his feet against the Arctic Pole.
You must not mind a certain coolness from him
Still said to haunt this side of Panther Mountain.
Nor need you mind the serial ordeal
Of being watched from forty cellar holes
As if by eye pairs out of forty firkins.
As for the woods' excitement over you
That sends light rustle rushes to their leaves,
Charge that to upstart inexperience.
Where were they all not twenty years ago?
They think too much of having shaded out
A few old pecker-fretted apple trees.
Make yourself up a cheering song of how
Someone's road home from work this once was,
Who may be just ahead of you on foot
Or creaking with a buggy load of grain.
The height of the adventure is the height
Of country where two village cultures faded
Into each other. Both of them are lost.
And if you're lost enough to find yourself
By now, pull in your ladder road behind you
And put a sign up CLOSED to all but me.
Then make yourself at home. The only field
Now left's no bigger than a harness gall.
First there's the children's house of make-believe,
Some shattered dishes underneath a pine,
The playthings in the playhouse of the children.
Weep for what little things could make them glad.
Then for the house that is no more a house,
But only a belilaced cellar hole,
Now slowly closing like a dent in dough.
This was no playhouse but a house in earnest.
Your destination and your destiny's

A brook that was the water of the house,
Cold as a spring as yet so near its source,
Too lofty and original to rage.
(We know the valley streams that when aroused
Will leave their tatters hung on barb and thorn.)
I have kept hidden in the instep arch
Of an old cedar at the waterside
A broken drinking goblet like the Grail
Under a spell so the wrong ones can't find it,
So can't get saved, as Saint Mark says they mustn't.
(I stole the goblet from the children's playhouse.)
Here are your waters and your watering place.
Drink and be whole again beyond confusion.

Thirty years ago, it reminded me of my dad, then in his seventies. Now it makes me think of age and death for us all. It came to me last weekend as I was going to the basement (scaring the cellar once in going there and again in clomping off).

—Carole Granger, 54, University Law Librarian, Missoula, Montana

An Old Man's Winter Night

All out-of-doors looked darkly in at him
Through the thin frost, almost in separate stars,
That gathers on the pane in empty rooms.
What kept his eyes from giving back the gaze
Was the lamp tilted near them in his hand.
What kept him from remembering what it was
That brought him to that creaking room was age.
He stood with barrels round him—at a loss.
And having scared the cellar under him
In clomping here, he scared it once again
In clomping off—and scared the outer night,
Which has its sounds, familiar, like the roar
Of trees and crack of branches, common things,
But nothing so like beating on a box.
A light he was to no one but himself

Where now he sat, concerned with he knew what,
A quiet light, and then not even that.
He consigned to the moon—such as she was,
So late-arising—to the broken moon,
As better than the sun in any case
For such a charge, his snow upon the roof,
His icicles along the wall to keep;
And slept. The log that shifted with a jolt
Once in the stove, disturbed him and he shifted,
And eased his heavy breathing, but still slept.
One aged man—one man—can't keep a house,
A farm, a countryside, or if he can,
It's thus he does it of a winter night.

I think a lot of kids don't get an opportunity to play, to use their imaginations—they're so hungry for it. The first time I ever read the poem " 'Out, Out—' " I was stunned by it. In the poem, the boy . . . his tragedy could have been avoided just by somebody saying, "Oh, call it a day. We're done. Go be a kid. Go play. Here's your time to play." And the kids that I work with—a lot of times they don't have the time for play, I fear.
—Elizabeth Wojtusik, 38, Teaching Artist, Humarock, Massachusetts

"Out, Out—" DVD, Track 14

The buzz saw snarled and rattled in the yard
And made dust and dropped stove-length sticks of wood,
Sweet-scented stuff when the breeze drew across it.
And from there those that lifted eyes could count
Five mountain ranges one behind the other
Under the sunset far into Vermont.
And the saw snarled and rattled, snarled and rattled,
As it ran light, or had to bear a load.
And nothing happened: day was all but done.
Call it a day, I wish they might have said
To please the boy by giving him the half hour
That a boy counts so much when saved from work.
His sister stood beside them in her apron

Robert Frost   79

To tell them "Supper." At the word, the saw,
As if to prove saws knew what supper meant,
Leaped out at the boy's hand, or seemed to leap—
He must have given the hand. However it was,
Neither refused the meeting. But the hand!
The boy's first outcry was a rueful laugh,
As he swung toward them holding up the hand,
Half in appeal, but half as if to keep
The life from spilling. Then the boy saw all—
Since he was old enough to know, big boy
Doing a man's work, though a child at heart—
He saw all spoiled. "Don't let him cut my hand off—
The doctor, when he comes. Don't let him, sister!"
So. But the hand was gone already.
The doctor put him in the dark of ether.
He lay and puffed his lips out with his breath.
And then—the watcher at his pulse took fright.
No one believed. They listened at his heart.
Little—less—nothing!—and that ended it.
No more to build on there. And they, since they
Were not the one dead, turned to their affairs.

The last line of this poem literally takes my breath away—there is a sense of something that has been irretrievably lost, or forever changed for the worse. I believe this poem speaks not only to our relationship with nature, but to our relationship with one another. Sometimes, we keep on singing, but our heart is heavy and we know we'll never be the same again. How do we turn tragedy and heartache into something positive? We keep on singing. Listen to the birds.

—Fredrick Johnson, 43, Quality Assurance Specialist, San Diego,
   California

The Oven Bird

There is a singer everyone has heard,
Loud, a mid-summer and a mid-wood bird,
Who makes the solid tree trunks sound again.

He says that leaves are old and that for flowers
Mid-summer is to spring as one to ten.
He says the early petal-fall is past,
When pear and cherry bloom went down in showers
On sunny days a moment overcast;
And comes that other fall we name the fall.
He says the highway dust is over all.
The bird would cease and be as other birds
But that he knows in singing not to sing.
The question that he frames in all but words
Is what to make of a diminished thing.

*This poem reminds me of when I was a boy: my grandfather would take
me with him to check on the cows or fix fences or just spend time together.
My mother was a single parent, my grandfather more of a father, and this
poem makes me think of them.*

—Jason Wolfe, 22, Student, Fort Collins, Colorado

The Pasture

I'm going out to clean the pasture spring;
I'll only stop to rake the leaves away
(And wait to watch the water clear, I may):
I shan't be gone long.—You come too.

I'm going out to fetch the little calf
That's standing by the mother. It's so young
It totters when she licks it with her tongue.
I shan't be gone long.—You come too.

ALLEN GINSBERG

UNITED STATES • 1926–1997

This poem reminds me of every reason I write, from an abiding marvel at the beauty of things to an equally abiding, and sometimes almost shameful, thirst for praise.

—Katerina Montaniel, 19, Student

Transcription of Organ Music

The flower in the glass peanut bottle formerly in the kitchen
    crooked to take a place in the light,
the closet door opened, because I used it before, it kindly stayed
    open waiting for me, its owner.

I began to feel my misery in pallet on floor, listening to music, my
    misery, that's why I want to sing.
The room closed down on me, I expected the presence of the
    Creator, I saw my gray painted walls and ceiling, they con-
    tained my room, they contained me
as the sky contained my garden,
I opened my door

       The rambler vine climbed up the cottage post, the leaves
in the night still where the day had placed them, the animal heads
of the flowers where they had arisen
       to think at the sun

       Can I bring back the words? Will thought of transcription
haze my mental open eye?

       The kindly search for growth, the gracious desire to exist
of the flowers, my near ecstasy at existing among them
       The privilege to witness my existence—you too must seek
the sun . . .

       My books piled up before me for my use
       waiting in space where I placed them, they haven't disap-
peared, time's left its remnants and qualities for me to use—my
words piled up, my texts, my manuscripts, my loves.
       I had a moment of clarity, saw the feeling in the heart of
things, walked out to the garden crying.

Saw the red blossoms in the night light, sun's gone, they
had all grown, in a moment, and were waiting stopped in time for
the day sun to come and give them . . .

Flowers which as in a dream at sunset I watered faithfully
not knowing how much I loved them.

I am so lonely in my glory—except they too out there—I
looked up—those red bush blossoms beckoning and peering in
the window waiting in blind love, their leaves too have hope and
are upturned top flat to the sky to receive—all creation open to
receive—the flat earth itself.

The music descends, as does the tall bending stalk of the
heavy blossom, because it has to, to stay alive, to continue to the
last drop of joy.

The world knows the love that's in its breast as in the
flower, the suffering lonely world.

The Father is merciful.

The light socket is crudely attached to the ceiling, after
the house was built, to receive a plug which sticks in it allright,
and serves my phonograph now . . .

The closet door is open for me, where I left it, since I left
it open, it has graciously stayed open.

The kitchen has no door, the hole there will admit me
should I wish to enter the kitchen.

I remember when I first got laid, H.P. graciously took my
cherry, I sat on the docks of Provincetown, age 23, joyful, elevated
in hope with the Father, the door to the womb was open to admit
me if I wished to enter.

There are unused electricity plugs all over my house if I
ever need them.

The kitchen window is open, to admit air . . .

The telephone—sad to relate—sits on the floor—I haven't
the money to get it connected—

I want people to bow as they see me and say he is gifted
with poetry, he has seen the presence of the Creator.

And the Creator gave me a shot of his presence to gratify
my wish, so as not to cheat me of my yearning for him.

Allen Ginsberg

LOUISE GLÜCK

UNITED STATES • B. 1943

*Raised on an Iowa farm, I walked to school each day through our apple
orchard. The abundance of apples meant that our teacher and my friends
in our one-room schoolhouse could have all the fruit they wanted. And my
mother "scoured" the orchard, canning "ammunition" for the long winter.*
—Fern Overvold, Retired English Teacher, Boca Raton, Florida

The School Children

The children go forward with their little satchels.
And all morning the mothers have labored
to gather the late apples, red and gold,
like words of another language.

And on the other shore
are those who wait behind great desks
to receive these offerings.

How orderly they are—the nails
on which the children hang
their overcoats of blue or yellow wool.

And the teachers shall instruct them in silence
and the mothers shall scour the orchards for a way out,
drawing to themselves the gray limbs of the fruit trees
bearing so little ammunition.

JOHANN WOLFGANG VON GOETHE

GERMANY • 1749–1842

My eldest daughter was a lover of gardens and gardening, and she planted in her garden the kind of shrubs like buddleia which attract butterflies. She died of cancer, and a few weeks after her committal in the Buddhist monastery, I was sitting in my garden and a butterfly flew and settled on my arm; and it didn't go away for quite a long time—you know how butterflies come and go very quickly—it just sat there, and I had the feeling that Gabriel had come to say "good-bye" to me.

—Olivia Milward, 74, Retired Teacher, San Francisco, California

The Holy Longing

DVD, Track 5

Tell a wise person, or else keep silent,
because the massman will mock it right away.
I praise what is truly alive,
what longs to be burned to death.

In the calm water of the love-nights,
where you were begotten, where you have begotten,
a strange feeling comes over you
when you see the silent candle burning.

Now you are no longer caught
in the obsession with darkness,
and a desire for higher love-making
sweeps you upward.

Distance does not make you falter,
now, arriving in magic, flying,
and, finally, insane for the light,
you are the butterfly and you are gone.

And so long as you haven't experienced
this: to die and so to grow,
you are only a troubled guest
on the dark earth.

Translated from the German by Robert Bly

Johann Wolfgang von Goethe

THOMAS GRAY

ENGLAND • 1716–1771

An ode to a house cat. Humor, wit, style—an ideal poem for those who love elegance and cats and the elegance of cats.

—Jo Allan Bradham, Marietta, Georgia

Ode on the Death of a Favorite Cat

Drowned in a Tub of Goldfishes

'Twas on a lofty vase's side,
Where China's gayest art had dyed
   The azure flowers that blow;
Demurest of the tabby kind,
The pensive Selima reclined,
   Gazed on the lake below.

Her conscious tail her joy declared;
The fair round face, the snowy beard,
   The velvet of her paws,
Her coat, that with the tortoise vies,
Her ears of jet, and emerald eyes,
   She saw; and purred applause.

Still had she gazed; but 'midst the tide
Two angel forms were seen to glide,
   The genii of the stream:
Their scaly armor's Tyrian hue
Through richest purple to the view
   Betrayed a golden gleam.

The hapless nymph with wonder saw:
A whisker first and then a claw,
   With many an ardent wish,
She stretched in vain to reach the prize.
What female heart can gold despise?
   What cat's averse to fish?

Presumptuous maid! with looks intent
Again she stretched, again she bent,

Nor knew the gulf between.
(Malignant Fate sat by and smiled)
The slipp'ry verge her feet beguiled,
    She tumbled headlong in.

Eight times emerging from the flood
She mewed to ev'ry watery god,
    Some speedy aid to send.
No dolphin came, no nereid stirred:
Nor cruel Tom, nor Susan heard,
    A fav'rite has no friend!

From hence, ye beauties, undeceived,
Know, one false step is ne'er retrieved,
    And be with caution bold.
Not all that tempts your wandering eyes
And heedless hearts is lawful prize;
    Nor all that glisters gold.

Thomas Gray

THOM GUNN

ENGLAND · B. 1929

Someone gains the trust of another, and they begin to take advantage of it.
I see things like that happen all around me every single day.
—Sarah M., 15, Student, Lincoln, Nebraska

The Idea of Trust

The idea of trust, or,
the thief. He
was always around,
"pretty" Jim.
Like a lilac bush or
a nice picture on the wall.
Blue eyes of an
intense vagueness
and the well-arranged
bearing of an animal.
Then one day he
said something
              he said
that trust is
an intimate conspiracy.

What did that
mean? Anyway next day
he was gone, with
all the money and dope
of the people he'd lived with.

I begin
to understand. I see him
picking through their things
at his leisure, with
a quiet secret smile
choosing and taking,
having first discovered
and set up his phrase to
scramble

that message of
enveloping trust.

He's getting
free. His eyes
are almost transparent.
He has put on
gloves. He fingers
the little privacies of those
who acted as if there
should be no privacy.

They took that
risk.
    Wild lilac
chokes the garden.

DONALD HALL

UNITED STATES • B. 1928

I tend to choose poems the same way I choose friends—the best ones teach me a great deal while I'm almost too busy laughing to notice.

—Pamela Ehrenberg, 26, Accreditation Associate, Washington, District of Columbia

Woolworth's

My whole life has led me here.

Daisies made out of resin,
hairnets and submarines,
sandwiches, diaries, green
garden chairs,
and a thousand boxes of cough drops.

Three hundred years ago I was hedging
and ditching in Devon.

I lacked freedom of worship,
and freedom to trade molasses
for rum, for slaves, for molasses.

"I will sail to Massachusetts
to build the Kingdom
of Heaven on Earth!"

The side of a hill
swung open.
It was Woolworth's!

I followed this vision to Boston.

Donald Hall

Mark Halliday

UNITED STATES • B. 1949

It connects us in a very simple way. It's comforting, disconcerting, funny, and harsh.

—Mark Hammer, 37, Austin, Texas

Population

Isn't it nice that everyone has a grocery list
except the very poor you hear about occasionally
we all have a grocery list on the refrigerator door;
at any given time there are thirty million lists in America
that say BREAD. Isn't it nice
not to be alone in this. Sometimes
you visit someone's house for the first time
and you spot the list taped up on a kitchen cabinet
and you think Yes, we're all in this together.
TOILET PAPER. No getting around it.
Nice to think of us all
unwrapping the new rolls at once,
forty thousand of us at any given moment.

Orgasm, of course, being the most vivid example: imagine
an electrified map wired to every American bed:
those little lights popping
on both sides of the Great Divide,
popping to beat the band. But
we never beat the band: within an hour or day
we're horny again, or hungry, or burdened with waste.
But isn't it nice not to be alone in
any of it; nice to be not noticeably responsible,
acquitted eternally in the rituals of the tribe:
it's only human! It's only human and that's not much.

So, aren't you glad we have such advanced farm machinery,
futuristic fertilizers, half a billion chickens
almost ready to die. Here come the loaves of bread for us
thup thup thup thup for all of us thup thup thup
except maybe the very poor

thup thup
and man all the cattle we can fatten up man,
there's no stopping our steaks. And that's why
we can make babies galore, baby:
let's get on with it. Climb aboard.
Let's be affirmative here, let's be pro-life for God's sake
how can life be wrong?
People *need* people and the happiest people are
surrounded with friendly flesh.
If you have ten kids they'll be so sweet—
ten really sweet kids! Have twelve!
What if there were 48 pro baseball teams,
you could see a damn lot more games!

And in this fashion we get away
from tragedy. Because tragedy comes when someone
gets too special. Whereas,
if forty thousand kitchen counters
on any given Sunday night
have notes on them that say
I CAN'T TAKE IT ANY MORE
I'M GONE, DON'T TRY TO FIND ME
you can feel how *your* note is
no big thing in America,
so, no *horrible* heartbreak,
it's more like a TV episode,
you've seen this whole plot lots of times
and everybody gets by—
you feel better already—
everybody gets by
and it's nice. It's a people thing.
You've got to admit it's nice.

Mark Halliday

THOMAS HARDY

ENGLAND · 1840–1928

All that it means to be human is summed up in this poem. I find it the ultimate Eulogy for that person who treasures and appreciates life in our natural world.

—Virginia Brady, Plattsburgh, New York

Afterwards

When the Present has latched its postern behind my tremulous stay,
   And the May month flaps its glad green leaves like wings,
Delicate-filmed as new-spun silk, will the neighbours say,
   "He was a man who used to notice such things"?

If it be in the dusk when, like an eyelid's soundless blink,
   The dewfall-hawk comes crossing the shades to alight
Upon the wind-warped upland thorn, a gazer may think,
   "To him this must have been a familiar sight."

If I pass during some nocturnal blackness, mothy and warm,
   When the hedgehog travels furtively over the lawn,
One may say, "He strove that such innocent creatures should
     come to no harm,
   But he could do little for them; and now he is gone."

If, when hearing that I have been stilled at last, they stand at the
     door,
   Watching the full-starred heavens that winter sees,
Will this thought rise on those who will meet my face no more,
   "He was one who had an eye for such mysteries"?

And will any say when my bell of quittance is heard in the gloom,
   And a crossing breeze cuts a pause in its outrollings,
Till they rise again, as they were a new bell's boom,
   "He hears it not now, but used to notice such things"?

The essence of this poem is as pertinent as the day Hardy wrote it: the unspoken tragedies and futility of war. It should be engraved as a reminder and posted at the door of all governments.

—Virginia Johnston, 82, Retired Teacher, Boca Raton, Florida

The Man He Killed

"Had he and I but met
    By some old ancient inn,
We should have sat us down to wet
    Right many a nipperkin!

"But ranged as infantry,
    And staring face to face,
I shot at him as he at me,
    And killed him in his place.

"I shot him dead because—
    Because he was my foe,
Just so: my foe of course he was;
    That's clear enough; although

"He thought he'd 'list, perhaps,
    Off-hand like—just as I—
Was out of work—had sold his traps—
    No other reason why.

"Yes; quaint and curious war is!
    You shoot a fellow down
You'd treat if met where any bar is,
    Or help to half-a-crown."

Thomas Hardy

ROBERT HASS

UNITED STATES • B. 1941

I grew up in a cold-water flat on the Lower East Side (now euphemistically called the East Village). My mother was illiterate, while my father could read a Yiddish newspaper. I am the seventh of twelve children. My love of poetry goes back as far as my memory. Poetry has sustained me through crises and it has enhanced my existence. Hass's line about a lover being unable to cure his lover's loneliness touches a chord in me. We are all alone in our experiences, no two individuals perceive life in the same way, and it is this knowledge that causes an unspeakable sadness in me.
—Pearl Melniker, 76, Psychologist, New York, New York

I get chills when I think of the "immense, illiterate, consoling angels."
—Mark Woodworth, 26, College Baseball Coach, San Diego, California

I first read this poem when I was sixteen; I didn't understand it then, but I thought it was very beautiful, and somehow disconcerting. Over the years it's come to be very important to me, with the way it addresses the limitations and the blessings of being human, and loving someone else.
—Karin Kross, 25, Technical Writer, Austin, Texas

Privilege of Being

Many are making love. Up above, the angels
in the unshaken ether and crystal of human longing
are braiding one another's hair, which is strawberry blond
and the texture of cold rivers. They glance
down from time to time at the awkward ecstasy—
it must look to them like featherless birds
splashing in the spring puddle of a bed—
and then one woman, she is about to come,
peels back the man's shut eyelids and says,
look at me, and he does. Or is it the man
tugging the curtain rope in that dark theater?
Anyway, they do, they look at each other;
two beings with evolved eyes, rapacious,

startled, connected at the belly in an unbelievably sweet
lubricious glue, stare at each other,
and the angels are desolate. They hate it. They shudder
     pathetically
like lithographs of Victorian beggars
with perfect features and alabaster skin hawking rags
in the lewd alleys of the novel.
All of creation is offended by this distress.
It is like the keening sound the moon makes sometimes,
rising. The lovers especially cannot bear it,
it fills them with unspeakable sadness, so that
they close their eyes again and hold each other, each
feeling the mortal singularity of the body
they have enchanted out of death for an hour or so,
and one day, running at sunset, the woman says to the man,
I woke up feeling so sad this morning because I realized
that you could not, as much as I love you,
dear heart, cure my loneliness,
wherewith she touched his cheek to reassure him
that she did not mean to hurt him with this truth.
And the man is not hurt exactly,
he understands that life has limits, that people
die young, fail at love,
fail of their ambitions. He runs beside her, he thinks
of the sadness they have gasped and crooned their way out of
coming, clutching each other with old, invented
forms of grace and clumsy gratitude, ready
to be alone again, or dissatisfied, or merely
companionable like the couples on the summer beach
reading magazine articles about intimacy between the sexes
to themselves, and to each other,
and to the immense, illiterate, consoling angels.

ROBERT HAYDEN

UNITED STATES • 1913–1980

As a grower of night-blooming cereus, I feel the poem captures that transcendent state of being one feels when nature puts on a dynamite show.
—Susan Cee Wineberg, 55, Historic Preservationist, Ann Arbor,
   Michigan

The Night-Blooming Cereus

    And so for nights
we waited, hoping to see
the heavy bud
    break into flower.

    On its neck-like tube
hooking down from the edge
of the leaf-branch
    nearly to the floor,

    the bud packed
tight with its miracle swayed
stiffly on breaths
    of air, moved

    as though impelled
by stirrings within itself.
It repelled as much
    as it fascinated me

    sometimes—snake,
eyeless bird head,
beak that would gape
    with grotesque life-squawk.

    But you, my dear,
conceded less to the bizarre
than to the imminence
    of bloom. Yet we agreed

　　　　　we ought
to celebrate the blossom,
paint ourselves, dance
　　　　in honor of

　　　　archaic mysteries
when it appeared. Meanwhile
we waited, aware
　　　　of rigorous design.

　　　　Backster's
polygraph, I thought,
would have shown
　　　　(as clearly as it had

　　　　a philodendron's
fear) tribal sentience
in the cactus, focused
　　　　energy of will.

　　　　That belling of
tropic perfume—that
signalling
　　　　not meant for us;

　　　　the darkness
cloyed with summoning
fragrance. We dropped
　　　　trivial tasks

　　　　and marvelling
beheld at last the achieved
flower. Its moonlight
　　　　petals were

　　　　still unfold-
ing, the spike fringe of the outer
perianth recessing
　　　　as we watched.

　　　　Lunar presence,
foredoomed, already dying,

it charged the room
    with plangency

    older than human
cries, ancient as prayers
invoking Osiris, Krishna,
    Tezcátlipóca.

    We spoke
in whispers when
we spoke
    at all . . .

SEAMUS HEANEY

IRELAND · B. 1939

The simple evocation of the bond that is forged in the quiet, shared moments has never been more beautifully shown. It resonates with me now, at a time when my mother's thoughts are evaporating into her own private cloud.

—Joan De Rosa, 67, Retired Teacher, Setauket, New York

from "Clearances"

3

When all the others were away at Mass
I was all hers as we peeled potatoes.
They broke the silence, let fall one by one
Like solder weeping off the soldering iron:
Cold comforts set between us, things to share
Gleaming in a bucket of clean water.
And again let fall. Little pleasant splashes
From each other's work would bring us to our senses.

So while the parish priest at her bedside
Went hammer and tongs at the prayers for the dying
And some were responding and some crying
I remembered her head bent towards my head
Her breath in mine, our fluent dipping knives—
Never closer the whole rest of our lives.

ANTHONY HECHT

UNITED STATES · B. 1923

The poem transports me out of myself back into myself. The ideas intersect with my thoughts as a scientist viewing my world. I see myself in a continuum of life in a vital universe. The sublime is everywhere—the beauty of a cell, the architecture of DNA, the complex organ systems of a mouse, a honeybee colony, thought, mind, the expanding universe, particle physics. We arrive on time when we realize that the sublime is always here, around us.

—Nan Roche, 48, Biologist/Laboratory Manager, College Park, Maryland

Prospects

We have set out from here for the sublime
Pastures of summer shade and mountain stream;
I have no doubt we shall arrive on time.

Is all the green of that enameled prime
A snapshot recollection or a dream?
We have set out from here for the sublime

Without provisions, without one thin dime,
And yet, for all our clumsiness, I deem
It certain that we shall arrive on time.

No guidebook tells you if you'll have to climb
Or swim. However foolish we may seem,
We have set out from here for the sublime

And must get past the scene of an old crime
Before we falter and run out of steam,
Riddled by doubt that we'll arrive on time.

Yet even in winter a pale paradigm
Of birdsong utters its obsessive theme.
We have set out from here for the sublime;
I have no doubt we shall arrive on time.

George Herbert

ENGLAND · 1593–1633

I love the kindness with which God calls the railing priest back, and that he answers. I think the feeling at the end is of an acceptance that comes from the comfort of knowing one's duty and doing it even when it seems very difficult.

—Sharon Ruiz, 43, Personnel Director, New York, New York

The Collar

I struck the board and cried, "No more;
      I will abroad!
  What? shall I ever sigh and pine?
My lines and life are free, free as the road,
    Loose as the wind, as large as store.
        Shall I be still in suit?
    Have I no harvest but a thorn
    To let me blood, and not restore
What I have lost with cordial fruit?
        Sure there was wine
  Before my sighs did dry it; there was corn
    Before my tears did drown it.
  Is the year only lost to me?
    Have I no bays to crown it,
No flowers, no garlands gay? All blasted?
        All wasted?
  Not so, my heart; but there is fruit,
    And thou hast hands.
  Recover all thy sigh-blown age
On double pleasures: leave thy cold dispute
Of what is fit and not. Forsake thy cage,
      Thy rope of sands,
Which petty thoughts have made, and made to thee
  Good cable, to enforce and draw,
      And be thy law,
  While thou didst wink and wouldst not see.
      Away! take heed;
      I will abroad.

Call in thy death's-head there; tie up thy fears.
    He that forbears
  To suit and serve his need,
    Deserves his load."
But as I raved and grew more fierce and wild
    At every word,
Methought I heard one calling, *Child!*
    And I replied, *My Lord.*

ZBIGNIEW HERBERT

POLAND • 1924–1998

*I think I believe in joy, redemption, and a way out—how can such a poem
steady me?*
—Patricia Corbus, 63, Sarasota, Florida

The Envoy of Mr Cogito

Go where those others went to the dark boundary
for the golden fleece of nothingness your last prize

go upright among those who are on their knees
among those with their backs turned and those toppled in the
    dust

you were saved not in order to live
you have little time you must give testimony

be courageous when the mind deceives you be courageous
in the final account only this is important

and let your helpless Anger be like the sea
whenever you hear the voice of the insulted and beaten

let your sister Scorn not leave you
for the informers executioners cowards—they will win
they will go to your funeral and with relief will throw a lump of
    earth
the woodborer will write your smoothed-over biography

and do not forgive truly it is not in your power
to forgive in the name of those betrayed at dawn

beware however of unnecessary pride
keep looking at your clown's face in the mirror
repeat: I was called—weren't there better ones than I

beware of dryness of heart love the morning spring
the bird with an unknown name the winter oak

light on a wall the splendour of the sky
they don't need your warm breath
they are there to say: no one will console you

be vigilant—when the light on the mountains gives the sign—
      arise and go
as long as blood turns in the breast your dark star

repeat old incantations of humanity fables and legends
because this is how you will attain the good you will not attain
repeat great words repeat them stubbornly
like those crossing the desert who perished in the sand

and they will reward you with what they have at hand
with the whip of laughter with murder on a garbage heap

go because only in this way will you be admitted to the company
      of cold skulls
to the company of your ancestors: Gilgamesh Hector Roland
the defenders of the kingdom without limit and the city of ashes

Be faithful Go

Translated from the Polish by John and Bogdana Carpenter

ROBERT HERRICK

ENGLAND • 1591–1674

I've loved this poem ever since my college days and have said these lines to myself every time I have the occasion to wear a formal gown.
—Mary Blair, 83, Homemaker, Urbana, Illinois

Upon Julia's Clothes

When as in silks my Julia goes,
Then, then (me thinks) how sweetly flows
That liquefaction of her clothes.

Next, when I cast mine eyes and see
That brave Vibration each way free;
O how that glittering taketh me!

GERARD MANLEY HOPKINS

ENGLAND · 1844–1889

The importance of not choosing not to be—I know how that feels, for there have been times that I felt I wanted not to be. As the poet expresses, perhaps it is actually God who we wrestle with, who gives us despair so we may see what we really are made of.

—Laura Pardike, 23, Pharmacy Student, Houston, Texas

Carrion Comfort

Not, I'll not, carrion comfort, Despair, not feast on thee;
Not untwist—slack they may be—these last strands of man
In me ór, most weary, cry *I can no more.* I can;
Can something, hope, wish day come, not choose not to be.

But ah, but O thou terrible, why wouldst thou rude on me
Thy wring-earth right foot rock? lay a lionlimb against me? scan
With darksome devouring eyes my bruisèd bones? and fan,
O in turns of tempest, me heaped there; me frantic to avoid thee
    and flee?

Why? That my chaff might fly; my grain lie, sheer and clear.
Nay in all that toil, that coil, since (seems) I kissed the rod,
Hand rather, my heart lo! lapped strength, stole joy, would laugh,
    cheer.

Cheer whóm though? The héro whose héaven-handling flúng me,
    fóot tród
Me? or mé that fóught him? O whích one? is it eách one? That
    níght, that year
Of now done darkness I wretch lay wrestling with (my God!) my
    God.

Back in 1926, I was roaming through the stacks of the Widener Library at Harvard. When I was walking through the section on English poetry of the nineteenth century, I just at random lifted my arm and picked a book off the shelf. It was attributed to an author I was not familiar with—Gerard Manley Hopkins. The page that I turned to and began to read was a page devoted to a poem called "God's Grandeur." I couldn't believe what I was reading. It really shook me, because it was unlike anything else I had ever read before. Suddenly that whole book became alive to me. It was filled with such a lyric passion; it was so fierce and eloquent, wounded and yet radiant, that I knew that it was speaking directly to me and giving me a hint of the kind of poetry that I would be dedicated to for the rest of my life.

—Stanley Kunitz, 97, Poet, New York, New York

God's Grandeur

DVD, Track 16

The world is charged with the grandeur of God.
    It will flame out, like shining from shook foil;
    It gathers to a greatness, like the ooze of oil
Crushed. Why do men then now not reck his rod?
Generations have trod, have trod, have trod;
    And all is seared with trade; bleared, smeared with toil;
    And wears man's smudge and shares man's smell: the soil
Is bare now, nor can foot feel, being shod.

And for all this, nature is never spent;
    There lives the dearest freshness deep down things;
And though the last lights off the black West went
    Oh, morning, at the brown brink eastward, springs—
Because the Holy Ghost over the bent
    World broods with warm breast and with ah! bright wings.

Gerard Manley Hopkins

Hopkins, whose poem became a curious part of my courtship, said his verse was more for the ear than the eye, less to be read than heard. There is no "less" with Hopkins; both are more. It is as much fun to look at his invented words as to hear their wonderfully strange sounds, melodies, textures, to grasp his wry rhythms. He surrounds a reader with rapturous pathos.

—Mary Forsmark, 83, Retired Social Worker, Birch Harbor, Maine

To seem the stranger lies my lot . . .

To seem the stranger lies my lot, my life
Among strangers. Father and mother dear,
Brothers and sisters are in Christ not near
And he my peace/my parting, sword and strife.

England, whose honour O all my heart woos, wife
To my creating thought, would neither hear
Me, were I pleading, plead nor do I: I wéar-
Y of idle a being but by where wars are rife.

I am in Ireland now; now I am at a thírd
Remove. Not but in all removes I can
Kind love both give and get. Only what word

Wisest my heart breeds dark heaven's baffling ban
Bars or hell's spell thwarts. This to hoard unheard,
Heard unheeded, leaves me a lonely began.

A. E. HOUSMAN

ENGLAND · 1859–1936

This slowly filtered into my consciousness over years of my father's reciting it. Isn't it true of all of us? We are always wiser than we were last year.
—Matthew Gold, 27, Portfolio Accountant, Sacramento, California

When I was one-and-twenty

(A Shropshire Lad 13)

When I was one-and-twenty
  I heard a wise man say,
"Give crowns and pounds and guineas
  But not your heart away;
Give pearls away and rubies
  But keep your fancy free."
But I was one-and-twenty,
  No use to talk to me.

When I was one-and-twenty
  I heard him say again,
"The heart out of the bosom
  Was never given in vain;
'Tis paid with sighs a plenty
  And sold for endless rue."
And I am two-and-twenty,
  And oh, 'tis true, 'tis true.

LANGSTON HUGHES

UNITED STATES • 1902–1967

This is what I would like to say to my three children—and what I wish I could do for them.

—Margaret Voss, 54, Public School Administrator, Salem, Massachusetts

The Dream Keeper

Bring me all of your dreams,
You dreamers,
Bring me all of your
Heart melodies
That I may wrap them
In a blue cloud-cloth
Away from the too-rough fingers
Of the world.

I walk around with a smile on my face at school and with friends, but I still have different thoughts running through my head. It's never stable, it's always going. My parents are originally from Cambodia, but I wasn't born in Cambodia; I was born in Thailand, because they were having this geno-cide—Pol Pot was killing Cambodian people. My parents thought: they can't—they're not going to give up (that's where I learned never to give up), they're going to get out, they're going to escape for their lives. . . . And we were lucky, we had family here already and so they helped us get to America. I feel guilty that, hey, I'm here free and I'm better off than a lot of people in Cambodia—a feeling I'm not free to let out. And that's what Langston Hughes was saying.

—Pov Chin, 16, Student, Stockton, California

Minstrel Man   DVD, Track 3

Because my mouth
Is wide with laughter
And my throat
Is deep with song,

You do not think
I suffer after
I have held my pain
So long?

Because my mouth
Is wide with laughter,
You do not hear
My inner cry?
Because my feet
Are gay with dancing,
You do not know
I die?

I grew up on the poor side of middle class. We lived in Syracuse, New York, and my parents' commitment to me sent me to college and law school. I think they believed their gifts to me were solely financial, intellectual, or imparting a work ethic, but their best gifts to me were the following: from my mother, the lesson of really listening to people and liking them, no matter who they were, until they force you to feel otherwise; and from my dad, deep shame whenever I start to think I'm better than anyone else. "Motto" reminds me of those lessons in a simple, melodic way. Having attended competitive, predominantly white schools and working in a competitive, predominantly white law firm doing a contentious job, I frequently need the reminder.
—Eulas Boyd, 27, Attorney, New York, New York

Motto

I play it cool
And dig all jive.
That's the reason
I stay alive.

My motto,
As I live and learn,
        is:
*Dig And Be Dug
In Return.*

RICHARD HUGO

UNITED STATES · 1923–1982

Hugo died the semester before I was to take his poetry class at the University of Montana. I got over it somehow, and went on to get a degree in history and a job that moved me away from Montana to the East Coast. I thought I had escaped my own private Philipsburg. Then a couple of years ago my father died and I went through a divorce. I felt the shock of recognition when I read this poem again and realized how portable Philipsburg was. My life had broken down and the last good kiss I had was years ago. My house rang empty and I was indeed talking to myself. But Hugo didn't leave me there and fortunately neither has life. There is a girl at the end of my story, too: my five-year-old daughter whose red hair lights the wall.

—Pamela Aakre Wright, 39, Research Historian, Silver Spring, Maryland

Degrees of Gray in Philipsburg

You might come here Sunday on a whim.
Say your life broke down. The last good kiss
you had was years ago. You walk these streets
laid out by the insane, past hotels
that didn't last, bars that did, the tortured try
of local drivers to accelerate their lives.
Only churches are kept up. The jail
turned 70 this year. The only prisoner
is always in, not knowing what he's done.

The principal supporting business now
is rage. Hatred of the various grays
the mountain sends, hatred of the mill,
The Silver Bill repeal, the best liked girls
who leave each year for Butte. One good
restaurant and bars can't wipe the boredom out.
The 1907 boom, eight going silver mines,
a dance floor built on springs—
all memory resolves itself in gaze,
in panoramic green you know the cattle eat
or two stacks high above the town,

two dead kilns, the huge mill in collapse
for fifty years that won't fall finally down.

Isn't this your life? That ancient kiss
still burning out your eyes? Isn't this defeat
so accurate, the church bell simply seems
a pure announcement: ring and no one comes?
Don't empty houses ring? Are magnesium
and scorn sufficient to support a town,
not just Philipsburg, but towns
of towering blondes, good jazz and booze
the world will never let you have
until the town you came from dies inside?

Say no to yourself. The old man, twenty
when the jail was built, still laughs
although his lips collapse. Someday soon,
he says, I'll go to sleep and not wake up.
You tell him no. You're talking to yourself.
The car that brought you here still runs.
The money you buy lunch with,
no matter where it's mined, is silver
and the girl who serves your food
is slender and her red hair lights the wall.

IKKYU

JAPAN • 1394–1481

The poem hits me with its excitement and, for me, real joy, that there is something deeper than any material trapping that is untouchable and wonderful—and it reminds me that that is where my focus should be (even though it inevitably wanders).
—Tim Munson, 29, Teacher, Studio City, California

My real dwelling

My real dwelling
Has no pillars
And no roof either
So rain cannot soak it
And wind cannot blow it down!

Translated from the Japanese by John Stevens

RANDALL JARRELL

UNITED STATES • 1914–1965

The Islands

Man, if I said once, "I know,"
Laugh at me, stuff in my angry mouth
Your rueful and foolish laughter. Man is a stone.

Lips own love; did I say once, "I love"?
I said a word. When the hands told they were love,
I bled and I was beautiful. Man is a knife.

When I said blood, I say I bled.
Is man no more than pain? Speak for me, scars.
Knife holds for me no blood but mine—

When I told I could wish for more than you,
Death, I was dreaming I had died.
Next year's skull perplexed me like a kiss,

I felt my veins contorted with the tongue
That ran through them like my world's crazy will;
My breath cracks into sleep, time eats my fat,

Friends fall and my mouths fail, I brim to death
—Man's hands were wishes, all my wives were iron,
Death shades me like a sword, and I am kissing—

I sweat to my sea like a floe; blue, blue
Were all the islands of my sleep, I wake, I see—
I saw as I lay dying that unbroken sea.

The Woman at the Washington Zoo

The saris go by me from the embassies.

Cloth from the moon. Cloth from another planet.
They look back at the leopard like the leopard.

And I. . . .
           this print of mine, that has kept its color
Alive through so many cleanings; this dull null
Navy I wear to work, and wear from work, and so
To my bed, so to my grave, with no
Complaints, no comment: neither from my chief,
The Deputy Chief Assistant, nor his chief—
Only I complain. . . . this serviceable
Body that no sunlight dyes, no hand suffuses
But, dome-shadowed, withering among columns,
Wavy beneath fountains—small, far-off, shining
In the eyes of animals, these beings trapped
As I am trapped but not, themselves, the trap,
Aging, but without knowledge of their age,
Kept safe here, knowing not of death, for death—
Oh, bars of my own body, open, open!

The world goes by my cage and never sees me.
And there come not to me, as come to these,
The wild beasts, sparrows pecking the llamas' grain,
Pigeons settling on the bears' bread, buzzards
Tearing the meat the flies have clouded. . . .
                        Vulture,
When you come for the white rat that the foxes left,
Take off the red helmet of your head, the black
Wings that have shadowed me, and step to me as man:
The wild brother at whose feet the white wolves fawn,
To whose hand of power the great lioness
Stalks, purring. . . .
                You know what I was,
You see what I am: change me, change me!

Randall Jarrell

ROBINSON JEFFERS

UNITED STATES · 1887–1962

I came across this poem forty years ago. It was important to me, as it gave me a different view of my dad's death. He was a navy pilot lost in the Pacific—a man I never met—whose death was a huge loss to his two children and his widow. At first I think I was irritated by Jeffers's words, but over time these lines have been a yardstick by which to measure the death of any man. Maybe a "good" poem is one whose message changes as the reader ages.

—Marc Marcussen, 55, Chemistry Teacher, Mansfield, Massachusetts

The Eye

The Atlantic is a stormy moat; and the Mediterranean,
The blue pool in the old garden,
More than five thousand years has drunk sacrifice
Of ships and blood, and shines in the sun; but here the Pacific—
Our ships, planes, wars are perfectly irrelevant.
Neither our present blood-feud with the brave dwarfs
Nor any future world-quarrel of westering
And eastering man, the bloody migrations, greed of power, clash
    of faiths—
Is a speck of dust on the great scale-pan.
Here from this mountain shore, headland beyond stormy head-
    land plunging like dolphins through the blue sea-smoke
Into pale sea—look west at the hill of water: it is half the planet:
    this dome, this half-globe, this bulging
Eyeball of water, arched over to Asia,
Australia and white Antarctica: those are the eyelids that never
    close; this is the staring unsleeping
Eye of the earth; and what it watches is not our wars.

EVAN JONES

JAMAICA • B. 1927

The poem is set in the mid-forties in Jamaica. The main person in the poem is a small farmer who ekes out a living in the very hard hillsides of Portland of Jamaica. He's proud of what he does, he knows who he is, and he's not afraid of facing anyone who wants to criticize him. I like it because of that expression of who a Jamaican is, but I also like it because it was one of the first attempts by any Jamaican to use the Jamaican Creole in a way that could have universal understanding.

—George Scott, 72, Businessman, Hartford, Connecticut

The Song of the Banana Man

DVD, Track 18

Touris, white man, wipin his face,
Met me in Golden Grove market place.
He looked at m'ol' clothes brown wid stain,
An soaked right through wid de Portlan rain,
He cas his eye, turn up his nose,
He says, "You're a beggar man, I suppose?"
He says, "Boy, get some occupation,
Be of some value to your nation."
   I said, "By God and dis big right han
   You mus recognize a banana man.

"Up in de hills, where de streams are cool,
An mullet an janga swim in de pool,
I have ten acres of mountain side,
An a dainty-foot donkey dat I ride,
Four Gros Michel, an four Lacatan,
Some coconut trees, and some hills of yam,
An I pasture on dat very same lan
Five she-goats an a big black ram,
   Dat, by God an dis big right han
   Is de property of a banana man.

"I leave m'yard early-mornin time
An set m'foot to de mountain climb,
I ben m'back to de hot-sun toil,

Evan Jones

119

An in'cutlass rings on de stony soil,
Ploughin an weedin, diggin an plantin
Till Massa Sun drop back o John Crow mountain,
Den home again in cool evenin time,
Perhaps whistling dis likkle rhyme,
  Praise God an m'big right han
  I will live an die a banana man.

"Banana day is my special day,
I cut my stems an I'm on m'way,
Load up de donkey, leave de lan
Head down de hill to banana stan,
When de truck comes roun I take a ride
All de way down to de harbour side—
Dat is de night, when you, touris man,
Would change your place wid a banana man,
  Yes, by God, an m'big right han
  I will live an die a banana man.

"De bay is calm, an de moon is bright
De hills look black for de sky is light,
Down at de dock is an English ship,
Restin after her ocean trip,
While on de pier is a monstrous hustle,
Tallymen, carriers, all in a bustle,
Wid stems on deir heads in a long black snake
Some singin de songs dat banana men make,
  Like, Praise God an m'big right han
  I will live an die a banana man.

"Den de payment comes, an we have some fun,
Me, Zekiel, Breda and Duppy Son.
Down at de bar near United Wharf
We knock back a white rum, bus a laugh,
Fill de empty bag for further toil
Wid saltfish, breadfruit, coconut oil.
Den head back home to m'yard to sleep,
A proper sleep dat is long an deep.
  Yes, by God, an m'big right han
  I will live an die a banana man.

Evan Jones

"So when you see dese ol clothes brown wid stain,
An soaked right through wid de Portlan rain,
Don't cas your eye nor turn your nose,
Don't judge a man by his patchy clothes,
I'm a strong man, a proud man, an I'm free,
Free as dese mountains, free as dis sea,
I know myself, an I know my ways,
An will sing wid pride to de end o my days
    Praise God an m'big right han
    I will live an die a banana man."

Evan Jones

BEN JONSON

ENGLAND · 1573–1637

*Ben Jonson's over-the-top promises in "Inviting a Friend to Supper" make
me laugh. Jonson paints the strange, imaginary delights awaiting enjoy-
ment, and even admits that he will "tell you of more, and lye, so you will
come." I also love the seventeenth-century spellings; they slow me down
enough to pay attention to each word, which makes it easier to "see" the
feast. I once sent this poem to some friends to invite them for dinner, and I
can tell you they accepted!*

—Jeremy Mauldin, 31, Program Manager, Atlanta, Georgia

Inviting a Friend to Supper

To night, grave sir, both my poore house, and I
        Doe equally desire your companie:
Not that we thinke us worthy such a ghest,
        But that your worth will dignifie our feast,
With those that come; whose grace may make that seeme
        Something, which, else, could hope for no esteeme.
It is the faire acceptance, Sir, creates
        The entertaynment perfect: not the cates.
Yet shall you have, to rectifie your palate,
        An olive, capers, or some better sallade
Ushring the mutton; with a short-leg'd hen,
        If we can get her, full of egs, and then,
Limons, and wine for sauce: to these, a coney
        Is not to be despair'd of, for our money;
And, though fowle, now, be scarce, yet there are clarkes,
        The skie not falling, thinke we may have larkes.
Ile tell you of more, and lye, so you will come:
        Of partrich, pheasant, wood-cock, of which some
May yet be there; and godwit, if we can:
        Knat, raile, and ruffe too. How so ere, my man
Shall reade a piece of *Virgil*, *Tacitus*,
        Livie, or of some better booke to us,
Of which wee'll speake our minds, amidst our meate;
        And Ile professe no verses to repeate:

To this, if ought appeare, which I know not of,
            That will the pastrie, not my paper, show of.
Digestive cheese, and fruit there sure will bee;
            But that, which most doth take my *Muse,* and mee,
Is a pure cup of rich *Canary*-wine,
            Which is the *Mermaids,* now, but shall be mine:
Of which had *Horace,* or *Anacreon* tasted,
            Their lives, as doe their lines, till now had lasted.
Tobacco, Nectar, or the *Thespian* spring,
            Are all but *Luthers* beere, to this I sing.
Of this we will sup free, but moderately,
            And we will have no *Pooly',* or *Parrot* by;
Nor shall our cups make any guiltie men:
            But, at our parting, we will be, as when
We innocently met. No simple word,
            That shall be utter'd at our mirthfull boord,
Shall make us sad next morning: or affright
            The libertie, that wee'll enjoy to night.

I hope that one day someone will love me enough to put me in that light.
—Jennifer C., Student, Oceanside, New York

Lovel's Song

It was a beauty that I saw,
    So pure, so perfect, as the frame
    Of all the universe was lame,
To that one figure, could I draw,
Or give least line of it a law!

A skein of silk without a knot!
    A fair march made without a halt!
    A curious form without a fault!
A printed book without a blot!
All beauty, and without a spot!

Ben Jonson   123

DONALD JUSTICE

UNITED STATES • B. 1925

I've never been a big poetry reader, but I recently came across "Men at Forty." I am quickly coming up on this important milestone.
—Fred Perry, 36, Marketing Manager, Palo Alto, California

Men at Forty

Men at forty
Learn to close softly
The doors to rooms they will not be
Coming back to.

At rest on a stair landing,
They feel it moving
Beneath them now like the deck of a ship,
Though the swell is gentle.

And deep in mirrors
They rediscover
The face of the boy as he practices tying
His father's tie there in secret,

And the face of that father,
Still warm with the mystery of lather.
They are more fathers than sons themselves now.
Something is filling them, something

That is like the twilight sound
Of the crickets, immense,
Filling the woods at the foot of the slope
Behind their mortgaged houses.

JOHN KEATS

ENGLAND • 1795–1821

I have felt its truth and power for seventy years.

—Evelyn Bayless, 89, Kennett Square, Pennsylvania

from *Endymion*

Book 1, Lines 1–33

A thing of beauty is a joy for ever:
Its loveliness increases; it will never
Pass into nothingness; but still will keep
A bower quiet for us, and a sleep
Full of sweet dreams, and health, and quiet breathing.
Therefore, on every morrow, are we wreathing
A flowery band to bind us to the earth,
Spite of despondence, of the inhuman dearth
Of noble natures, of the gloomy days,
Of all the unhealthy and o'er-darkened ways
Made for our searching: yes, in spite of all,
Some shape of beauty moves away the pall
From our dark spirits. Such the sun, the moon,
Trees old, and young sprouting a shady boon
For simple sheep; and such are daffodils
With the green world they live in; and clear rills
That for themselves a cooling covert make
'Gainst the hot season; the mid forest brake,
Rich with a sprinkling of fair musk-rose blooms:
And such too is the grandeur of the dooms
We have imagined for the mighty dead;
All lovely tales that we have heard or read:
An endless fountain of immortal drink,
Pouring unto us from the heaven's brink.

Nor do we merely feel these essences
For one short hour; no, even as the trees
That whisper round a temple become soon
Dear as the temple's self, so does the moon,
The passion poesy, glories infinite,

Haunt us till they become a cheering light
Unto our souls, and bound to us so fast,
That, whether there be shine, or gloom o'ercast,
They alway must be with us, or we die.

*I have always believed the idea of romantic love needed a little salt. Keats
provides it here.*

—Phil Morse, 57, Design Artist, Cambridge, Massachusetts

On a Leander Which Miss Reynolds, My Kind Friend, Gave Me

Come hither all sweet maidens, soberly
Down-looking—aye, and with a chastened light
Hid in the fringes of your eyelids white—
And meekly let your fair hands joined be.
So gentle are ye that ye could not see,
Untouched, a victim of your beauty bright—
Sinking away to his young spirit's night,
Sinking bewildered mid the dreary sea:
'Tis young Leander toiling to his death.
Nigh swooning, he doth purse his weary lips
For Hero's cheek and smiles against her smile.
O horrid dream—see how his body dips
Dead heavy—arms and shoulders gleam awhile:
He's gone—up bubbles all his amorous breath.

It's beautiful description of something we all do and may not appreciate as a kind of daily gift of peace in a very hectic world.

—Laurel Burns, 47, Banker, Northridge, California

To Sleep

O soft embalmer of the still midnight,
Shutting, with careful fingers and benign,
Our gloom-pleased eyes, embowered from the light,
Enshaded in forgetfulness divine:
O soothest Sleep! If so it please thee, close
In midst of this thine hymn my willing eyes,
Or wait the "Amen," ere thy poppy throws
Around my bed its lulling charities.
Then save me, or the passed day will shine
Upon my pillow, breeding many woes,—
Save me from curious Conscience, that still lords
Its strength for darkness, burrowing like a mole;
Turn the key deftly in the oiled wards,
And seal the hushed Casket of my soul.

John Keats

JANE KENYON

UNITED STATES • 1947–1995

I, too, moved from another area of the country into a very old house. While the rest of the family was away at work and school I was very lonely. I busied myself polishing the wavy glass windows, scrubbing worn floors, and rescuing blue canning jars and old crockery from the musty cellar. I began to feel more and more comfortable, until one day I joined the ranks of women who have made this house a home.

—Beverly Zeigler White, 65, Instructional Aide, Kenton, Ohio

Finding a Long Gray Hair

I scrub the long floorboards
in the kitchen, repeating
the motions of other women
who have lived in this house.
And when I find a long gray hair
floating in the pail,
I feel my life added to theirs.

KENNETH KOCH

UNITED STATES · 1925–2002

Poets write of sunsets, skylarks, ships, the sea—but boiling water? I am intrigued that anyone can take such an ordinary concept and find so many other concepts that pertain in meaningful ways. It fascinates me. I live in a retirement center. Several years ago a group of us decided to see what we could learn about poetry, a sort of a "blind leading the blind" project. It has been a great experience.

—Madalene Barnett, 83, Retired, Newville, Pennsylvania

The Boiling Water

A serious moment for the water is when it boils
And though one usually regards it merely as a convenience
To have the boiling water available for bath or table
Occasionally there is someone around who understands
The importance of this moment for the water—maybe a saint,
Maybe a poet, maybe a crazy man, or just someone temporarily
        disturbed
With his mind "floating," in a sense, away from his deepest
Personal concerns to more "unreal" things. A lot of poetry
Can come from perceptions of this kind, as well as a lot of insane
        conversations.
Intense people can sometimes get stuck on topics like these
And keep you far into the night with them. Still, it is true
That the water has just started to boil. How important
For the water! And now I see that the tree is waving in the wind
(I assume it is the wind)—at least, its branches are. In order to see
Hidden meanings, one may have to ignore
The most exciting ones, those that are most directly appealing
And yet it is only these appealing ones that, often, one can trust
To make one's art solid and true, just as it is sexual attraction
One has to trust, often, in love. So the boiling water's seriousness
Is likely to go unobserved until the exact strange moment
(And what a temptation it is to end the poem here
With some secret thrust) when it involuntarily comes into the mind
And then one can write of it. A serious moment for this poem will
        be when it ends,

It will be like the water's boiling, that for which we've waited
Without trying to think of it too much, since "a watched pot never
   boils,"
And a poem with its ending figured out is difficult to write.

Once the water is boiling, the heater has a choice: to look at it
And let it boil and go on seeing what it does, or to take it off and
   use the water for tea,
Chocolate, or coffee, or beef consommé. You don't drink the
   product then
Until the water has ceased to boil, for otherwise
It would burn your tongue. Even hot water is dangerous and has a
   thorn
Like the rose, or a horn like the baby ram. Modest hot water, and
   the tree
Blowing in the wind. The connection here is how serious is it for
   the tree
To have its arms wave (its branches)? How did it ever get such
   flexibility
In the first place? and who put the boiling potentiality into water?
A tree will not boil, nor will the wind. Think of the dinners
We could have, and the dreams, if only they did.
But that is not to think of what things are really about. For the tree
I don't know how serious it is to be waving, though water's boiling
Is more dramatic, is more like a storm, high tide
And the ship goes down, but it comes back up as coffee, chocolate,
   or tea.

How many people I have drunk tea or coffee with
And thought about the boiling water hardly at all, just waiting for
   it to boil
So there could be coffee or chocolate or tea. And then what?
The body stimulated, the brain alarmed, grounds in the pot,
The tree, waving, out the window, perhaps with a little more élan
Because we saw it that way, because the water boiled, because we
   drank tea.

The water boils almost every time the same old way
And still it is serious, because it is boiling. That is what,
I think, one should see. From this may come compassion,

Kenneth Koch

Compassion and a knowledge of nature, although most of the time
I know I am not going to think about it. It would be crazy
To give such things precedence over such affairs of one's life
As involve more fundamental satisfactions. But is going to the
    beach
More fundamental than seeing the water boil? Saving of money,
It's well known, can result from an aesthetic attitude, since a rock
Picked up in the street contains all the shape and hardness of the
    world.
One sidewalk leads everywhere. You don't have to be in Estapan.

A serious moment for the island is when its trees
Begin to give it shade, and another is when the ocean washes
Big heavy things against its side. One walks around and looks at
    the island
But not really at it, at what is on it, and one thinks,
It must be serious, even, to be this island, at all, here,
Since it is lying here exposed to the whole sea. All its
Moments might be serious. It is serious, in such windy weather, to
    be a sail
Or an open window, or a feather flying in the street.

Seriousness, how often I have thought of seriousness
And how little I have understood it, except this: serious is urgent
And it has to do with change. You say to the water,
It's not necessary to boil now, and you turn it off. It stops
Fidgeting. And starts to cool. You put your hand in it
And say, The water isn't serious any more. It has the potential,
However—that urgency to give off bubbles, to
Change itself to steam. And the wind,
When it becomes part of a hurricane, blowing up the beach
And the sand dunes can't keep it away.
Fainting is one sign of seriousness, crying is another.
Shuddering all over is another one.

A serious moment for the telephone is when it rings,
And a person answers, it is Angelica, or is it you
And finally, at last, who answer, my wing, my past, my
Angel, my flume, and my de-control, my orange and my good-bye
    kiss,

Kenneth Koch   131

My extravagance, and my weight at fifteen years old
And at the height of my intelligence, oh Cordillera two
And sandals one, C'est toi à l'appareil? Is that you at
The telephone, and when it snows, a serious moment for the bus is
    when it snows
For then it has to slow down for sliding, and every moment is a trust.

A serious moment for the fly is when its wings
Are moving, and a serious moment for the duck
Is when it swims, when it first touches water, then spreads
Its smile upon the water, its feet begin to paddle, it is in
And above the water, pushing itself forward, a duck.
And a serious moment for the sky is when, completely blue,
It feels some clouds coming; another when it turns dark.
A serious moment for the match is when it bursts into flame
And is all alone, living, in that instant, that beautiful second for
    which it was made.
So much went into it! The men at the match factory, the mood of
The public, the sand covering the barn
So it was hard to find the phosphorus, and now this flame,
This pink white ecstatic light blue! For the telephone when it rings,
For the wind when it blows, and for the match when it bursts into
    flame.

Serious, all our life is serious, and we see around us
Seriousness for other things, that touches us and seems as if it
    might be giving clues.
The seriousness of the house when it is being built
And is almost completed, and then the moment when it is
    completed.
The seriousness of the bee when it stings. We say, He has taken his
    life,
Merely to sting. Why would he do that? And we feel
We aren't concentrated enough, not pure, not deep
As the buzzing bee. The bee flies into the house
And lights on a chair arm and sits there, waiting for something to be
Other than it is, so he can fly again. He is boiling, waiting. Soon he
    is forgotten
And everyone is speaking again.

Kenneth Koch

Seriousness, everyone speaks of seriousness
Certain he knows or seeking to know what it is. A child is bitten
    by an animal
And that is serious. The doctor has a serious life. He is somewhat,
    in that, like the bee.
And water! water—how it is needed! and it is always going down
Seeking its own level, evaporating, boiling, now changing into ice
And snow, now making up our bodies. We drink the coffee
And somewhere in this moment is the chance
We will never see each other again. It is serious for the tree
To be moving, the flexibility of its moving
Being the sign of its continuing life. And now there are its blossoms
And the fact that it is blossoming again, it is filling up with
Pink and whitish blossoms, it is full of them, the wind blows, it is
Warm, though, so much is happening, it is spring, the people step
    out
And doors swing in, and billions of insects are born. You call me
    and tell me
You feel your life isn't worth living. I say that I'm coming to see
    you. I put the key in
And the car begins to clatter, and now it starts.

Serious for me that I met you, and serious for you
That you met me, and that we do not know
If we will ever be close to anyone again. Serious the recognition of
    the probability
That we will, although time stretches terribly in between. It is
    serious not to know
And to know and to try to figure things out. One's legs
Cross, foot swings, and a cigarette is blooming, a gray bouquet,
    and
The water is boiling. Serious the birth (what a phenomenon!) of
    anything and
The movements of the trees, and for the lovers
Everything they do and see. Serious intermittently for consciousness
The sign that something may be happening, always, today,
That is enough. For the germ when it enters or leaves a body. For
    the fly when it lifts its little wings.

Yusef Komunyakaa

UNITED STATES • B. 1947

I first read Yusef Komunyakaa's "Facing It" in Best American Poems. *For me as a veteran, it's a poem that pays tribute to all the veterans. I was in Vietnam in '65 for six months with a tactical fighter unit—F100 pilots. I had not been able to face the wall, and the poem helped me unlock my emotions. It captures, I think, the feelings of a lot of us, but it also interprets the monument, the memorial, for others—to help us see the integration of our atmosphere and our memories, as well as that sea of names.*

—Michael H. Lythgoe, 58, Foundation Director, Washington, District of Columbia

Facing It   DVD, Track 7

My black face fades,
hiding inside the black granite.
I said I wouldn't,
dammit: No tears.
I'm stone. I'm flesh.
My clouded reflection eyes me
like a bird of prey, the profile of night
slanted against morning. I turn
this way—the stone lets me go.
I turn that way—I'm inside
the Vietnam Veterans Memorial
again, depending on the light
to make a difference.
I go down the 58,022 names,
half-expecting to find
my own in letters like smoke.
I touch the name Andrew Johnson;
I see the booby trap's white flash.
Names shimmer on a woman's blouse
but when she walks away
the names stay on the wall.
Brushstrokes flash, a red bird's
wings cutting across my stare.

The sky. A plane in the sky.
A white vet's image floats
closer to me, then his pale eyes
look through mine. I'm a window.
He's lost his right arm
inside the stone. In the black mirror
a woman's trying to erase names:
No, she's brushing a boy's hair.

MAXINE KUMIN

UNITED STATES · B. 1925

In the moment that the speaker rides on her horse, she realizes they'll both die, and asks herself what she wants—not money, not fame, just the smell of garlic in a pan as she cooks for those she loves. The stunning brutal ending hits the reader like a bullet. What a poem.

—Candide Jones, 50, Restaurant Critic/Assistant University Press Director,
    Winston-Salem, North Carolina

Thinking of Death and Dogfood

Amanda, you'll be going
to Alpo or to Gaines
when you run out of luck;
the flesh flensed from your bones
your mammoth rib cage rowing
away to the renderer's
a dry canoe on a truck

while I foresee my corpse
slid feet first into fire
light as the baker's loaf
to make of me at least
a pint of potash spoor.
I'm something to sweeten the crops
when the clock hand stops.

Amanda, us in the woods
miles from home, the ground
upending in yellow flutes
that open but make no sound.
Ferns in the mouth of the brute,
chanterelles in the woman's sack . . .
what do I want for myself
dead center, bareback
on the intricate harp of your spine?
All that I name as mine

with the sure slow oxen of words:
feed sacks as grainy as boards
that air in the sun. A boy
who is wearing my mother's eyes.
Garlic to crush in the pan.
The family gathering in.
Already in the marsh
the yearling maples bleed
a rich onrush. Time slips
another abacus bead.

Let it not stick in the throat
or rattle a pane in the mind.
May I leave no notes behind
wishful, banal or occult
and you, small thinker in
the immensity of your frame
may you be caught and crammed
midmouthful of the best grain
when the slaughterer's bullet slams
sidelong into your brain.

STANLEY KUNITZ

UNITED STATES • B. 1905

When I read the poem for the first time, I read the first five lines and I immediately burst into tears, because it reflected something about myself that I have never articulated or thought about clearly, but it was so deeply true. As I continued reading, it got very dark and toward the end it made me laugh. I think that a poem that is true to the essence and can make you laugh is extraordinary.

—Donna Bickel, 62, Bookkeeper, Larkspur, California

Hornworm: Autumn Lamentation

DVD, Track 17

Since that first morning when I crawled
into the world, a naked grubby thing,
and found the world unkind,
my dearest faith has been that this
is but a trial: I shall be changed.
In my imaginings I have already spent
my brooding winter underground,
unfolded silky powdered wings, and climbed
into the air, free as a puff of cloud
to sail over the steaming fields,
alighting anywhere I pleased,
thrusting into deep tubular flowers.

It is not so: there may be nectar
in those cups, but not for me.
All day, all night, I carry on my back
embedded in my flesh, two rows
of little white cocoons,
so neatly stacked
they look like eggs in a crate.
And I am eaten half away.

If I can gather strength enough
I'll try to burrow under a stone
and spin myself a purse
in which to sleep away the cold;
though when the sun kisses the earth

again, I know I won't be there.
Instead, out of my chrysalis
will break, like robbers from a tomb,
a swarm of parasitic flies,
leaving my wasted husk behind.

Sir, you with the red snippers
in your hand, hovering over me,
casting your shadow, I greet you,
whether you come as an angel of death
or of mercy. But tell me,
before you choose to slice me in two:
Who can understand the ways
of the Great Worm in the Sky?

*I find myself turning to this poem in times of extreme happiness and sad-
ness, transitions, milestones, death. Kunitz, at the same time, consoles me
and toughens me for the journey.*
—Judith M. Ferrara, 55, Visual Artist/Writer, Worcester, Massachusetts

*The older I am, the more the poem means to me—more a companion than
a consolation.*
—Mary Emerson-Smith, 58, Family Therapist, Atlantic Beach, Florida

*After I went through a divorce and several job changes and finally became
more peacefully retrospective, this poem initially moved me to the point of
tears, and continues to do so every time I read it, quietly or aloud. It is,
knowingly or unknowingly, relevant to all of us who breathe.*
—Bob Williams, 53, Advertising Professional, Indianapolis, Indiana

The Layers

I have walked through many lives,
some of them my own,
and I am not who I was,
though some principle of being
abides, from which I struggle

not to stray.
When I look behind,
as I am compelled to look
before I can gather strength
to proceed on my journey,
I see the milestones dwindling
toward the horizon
and the slow fires trailing
from the abandoned camp-sites,
over which scavenger angels
wheel on heavy wings.
Oh, I have made myself a tribe
out of my true affections,
and my tribe is scattered!
How shall the heart be reconciled
to its feast of losses?
In a rising wind
the manic dust of my friends,
those who fell along the way,
bitterly stings my face.
Yet I turn, I turn,
exulting somewhat,
with my will intact to go
wherever I need to go,
and every stone on the road
precious to me.
In my darkest night,
when the moon was covered
and I roamed through wreckage,
a nimbus-clouded voice
directed me:
"Live in the layers,
not on the litter."
Though I lack the art
to decipher it,
no doubt the next chapter
in my book of transformations
is already written.
I am not done with my changes.

Philip Larkin

ENGLAND • 1922–1985

It cuts to what human beings want to believe and will believe given the encouragement and despite any evidence to the contrary: that love is immortal.

—Joan Smith, 53, Art Director, Boxborough, Massachusetts

An Arundel Tomb

Side by side, their faces blurred,
The earl and countess lie in stone,
Their proper habits vaguely shown
As jointed armour, stiffened pleat,
And that faint hint of the absurd—
The little dogs under their feet.

Such plainness of the pre-baroque
Hardly involves the eye, until
It meets his left-hand gauntlet, still
Clasped empty in the other; and
One sees, with a sharp tender shock,
His hand withdrawn, holding her hand.

They would not think to lie so long.
Such faithfulness in effigy
Was just a detail friends would see:
A sculptor's sweet commissioned grace
Thrown off in helping to prolong
The Latin names around the base.

They would not guess how early in
Their supine stationary voyage
The air would change to soundless damage,
Turn the old tenantry away;
How soon succeeding eyes begin
To look, not read. Rigidly they

Persisted, linked, through lengths and breadths
Of time. Snow fell, undated. Light

Each summer thronged the glass. A bright
Litter of birdcalls strewed the same
Bone-riddled ground. And up the paths
The endless altered people came,

Washing at their identity.
Now, helpless in the hollow of
An unarmorial age, a trough
Of smoke in slow suspended skeins
Above their scrap of history,
Only an attitude remains:

Time has transfigured them into
Untruth. The stone fidelity
They hardly meant has come to be
Their final blazon, and to prove
Our almost-instinct almost true:
What will survive of us is love.

The Explosion

On the day of the explosion
Shadows pointed towards the pithead:
In the sun the slagheap slept.

Down the lane came men in pitboots
Coughing oath-edged talk and pipe-smoke,
Shouldering off the freshened silence.

One chased after rabbits; lost them;
Came back with a nest of lark's eggs;
Showed them; lodged them in the grasses.

So they passed in beards and moleskins,
Fathers, brothers, nicknames, laughter,
Through the tall gates standing open.

At noon, there came a tremor; cows
Stopped chewing for a second; sun,
Scarfed as in a heat-haze, dimmed.

The dead go on before us, they
Are sitting in God's house in comfort,
We shall see them face to face—

Plain as lettering in the chapels
It was said, and for a second
Wives saw men of the explosion

Larger than in life they managed—
Gold as on a coin, or walking
Somehow from the sun towards them,

One showing the eggs unbroken.

Philip Larkin   143

DENISE LEVERTOV

UNITED STATES • 1923–1997

It seems whenever I have something I'd like to express out loud, I am that clodhopper, clumsily breaking into the gliding ring of conversation. I grew up on a farm, where I'd relish my time with the animals, and as a child wrote poetry in the silent barn and can feel myself there again when I read the poem. It gives me the chilling hope that someday, when my surroundings are calm, and I quietly write, the muse will suddenly reach into my throat and pull my voice into the ring of dance.

—Ingrid Ankerson, 25, Crab Girl (Seasonal), Baltimore, Maryland

Caedmon

All others talked as if
talk were a dance.
Clodhopper I, with clumsy feet
would break the gliding ring.
Early I learned to
hunch myself
close by the door:
then when the talk began
I'd wipe my
mouth and wend
unnoticed back to the barn
to be with the warm beasts,
dumb among body sounds
of the simple ones.
I'd see by a twist
of lit rush the motes
of gold moving
from shadow to shadow
slow in the wake
of deep untroubled sighs.
The cows
munched or stirred or were still. I
was at home and lonely
both in good measure. Until

the sudden angel affrighted me—light effacing
my feeble beam,
a forest of torches, feathers of flame, sparks upflying:
but the cows as before
were calm, and nothing was burning,
　　　　nothing but I, as that hand of fire
touched my lips and scorched my tongue
and pulled my voice
　　　　　　　　into the ring of the dance.

PHILIP LEVINE

UNITED STATES · B. 1928

This poem enabled me to see that poetry was about real people. It brought home the message that one's racial hatred for others is closely connected to one's own self-loathing. Poetry is the internal music of pain.
—Dean Smith, 37, Sales Director, Alexandria, Virginia

I feed and I lion.
—John Rubio, 24, Teacher, Oceanside, California

They Feed They Lion

Out of burlap sacks, out of bearing butter,
Out of black bean and wet slate bread,
Out of the acids of rage, the candor of tar,
Out of creosote, gasoline, drive shafts, wooden dollies,
They Lion grow.
          Out of the gray hills
Of industrial barns, out of rain, out of bus ride,
West Virginia to Kiss My Ass, out of buried aunties,
Mothers hardening like pounded stumps, out of stumps,
Out of the bones' need to sharpen and the muscles' to stretch,
They Lion grow.
          Earth is eating trees, fence posts,
Gutted cars, earth is calling in her little ones,
"Come home, Come home!" From pig balls,
From the ferocity of pig driven to holiness,
From the furred ear and the full jowl come
The repose of the hung belly, from the purpose
They Lion grow.
          From the sweet glues of the trotters
Come the sweet kinks of the fist, from the full flower
Of the hams the thorax of caves,
From "Bow Down" come "Rise Up,"
Come they Lion from the reeds of shovels,
The grained arm that pulls the hands,
They Lion grow.

From my five arms and all my hands,
From all my white sins forgiven, they feed,
From my car passing under the stars,
They Lion, from my children inherit,
From the oak turned to a wall, they Lion,
From they sack and they belly opened
And all that was hidden burning on the oil-stained earth
They feed they Lion and he comes.

The poem evokes the Detroit that shadowed my childhood, growing up in its suburbs, the Detroit that is still visible today: hard work, the scent of metal, a stooped but proud back. I can hear the man speaking, see the desperation in his face. The poem tells a story, but with restraint. It leaves you wondering about this man, his life. Is it more than the act of working? There was a time in my life when I did not understand the poem's power, and I feel I came to a breakthrough when it actually hit me. It was a moment of growth for me, one I can pinpoint precisely.
—Mechelle Zarou, 27, Attorney, Perrysburg, Ohio

What Work Is

We stand in the rain in a long line
waiting at Ford Highland Park. For work.
You know what work is—if you're
old enough to read this you know what
work is, although you may not do it.
Forget you. This is about waiting,
shifting from one foot to another.
Feeling the light rain falling like mist
into your hair, blurring your vision
until you think you see your own brother
ahead of you, maybe ten places.
You rub your glasses with your fingers,
and of course it's someone else's brother,
narrower across the shoulders than
yours but with the same sad slouch, the grin

that does not hide the stubbornness,
the sad refusal to give in to
rain, to the hours wasted waiting,
to the knowledge that somewhere ahead
a man is waiting who will say, "No,
we're not hiring today," for any
reason he wants. You love your brother,
now suddenly you can hardly stand
the love flooding you for your brother,
who's not beside you or behind or
ahead because he's home trying to
sleep off a miserable night shift
at Cadillac so he can get up
before noon to study his German.
Works eight hours a night so he can sing
Wagner, the opera you hate most,
the worst music ever invented.
How long has it been since you told him
you loved him, held his wide shoulders,
opened your eyes wide and said those words,
and maybe kissed his cheek? You've never
done something so simple, so obvious,
not because you're too young or too dumb,
not because you're jealous or even mean
or incapable of crying in
the presence of another man, no,
just because you don't know what work is.

Philip Levine

VACHEL LINDSAY

UNITED STATES • 1879–1931

My relationship to the poetry of Vachel Lindsay, as his son, is to have joined with my mother in paying off the debts he incurred in fashioning it. I started wage-working at thirteen and we got them paid off a few months before I married, at eighteen, in 1945. I give my hearty allegiance to his quest, to his work, to his excellent achievement. I find this particular poem to be a big help in tough times (burying our first son, or buckling back down to wage work again when it had once seemed we'd be able to do art). The spring, the powerfully erotic buffaloes, the Pawnees—these are not overcome. Not dead. Just lying low. What excellent modesty on the part of the poet. The very truth of our grief's redemption.

—Nick Lindsay, 74, Carpenter, Edisto Island, South Carolina

The Flower-Fed Buffaloes

The flower-fed buffaloes of the spring
In the days of long ago,
Ranged where the locomotives sing
And the prairie flowers lie low:—
The tossing, blooming, perfumed grass
Is swept away by the wheat,
Wheels and wheels and wheels spin by
In the spring that still is sweet.
But the flower-fed buffaloes of the spring
Left us, long ago.
They gore no more, they bellow no more,
They trundle around the hills no more:—
With the Blackfeet, lying low,
With the Pawnees, lying low,
Lying low.

LI PO

CHINA · 701–762

It is a very well-known poem to the Chinese people and everyone loves it.
Whenever I hear or read it, I think of my hometown.

—Anna Hsu, 10, Student, Orlando, Florida

Still Night Thoughts

Moonlight in front of my bed—
I took it for frost on the ground!
I lift my eyes to watch the mountain moon,
lower them and dream of home.

Translated from the Chinese by Burton Watson

Liu Zongyuan

CHINA · 773–819

Liu Zongyuan was a statesman, activist for political reform, and a poet. His poems and political philosophy brought important impact in the political and literary arena of the T'ang Dynasty. This poem depicts Liu's inner tranquillity while dealing with the tremendous turmoil in the outside world.

—Judy Lu, 45, Librarian, Washington, District of Columbia

River-Snow

A hundred mountains and no bird,
A thousand paths without a footprint;
A little boat, a bamboo cloak,
An old man fishing in the cold river-snow.

Translated from the Chinese by Witter Bynner

Henry Wadsworth Longfellow

UNITED STATES • 1807–1882

I was born in Roxbury Crossing on the threshold of the Great Depression. My parents were Afro-Caribbean immigrants from the island of Barbados. The Great Depression brought difficult times in our family—exposed us to public welfare, poverty, fear, and a lot of other things. My father's hopes of gold in America became depressed and became a part of the oppression of racism that could impose itself upon a man of color at that time in history. So I grew up poor, but I grew up seeking for some faith and hope. In junior high school, an Irish teacher kept quoting verses from Longfellow: "Be not like dumb, driven cattle! / Be a hero in the strife!" At that time I didn't understand all that it was really saying, but I learned it and it stayed in my mind. Later on, feeling called to the Christian Ministry, as a theological student, this "Psalm of Life" began to take on real meaning for me in my own personal struggles in life and as I looked back and reflected upon my childhood and the experiences of my parents.

—Michael Haynes, 71, Minister, Roxbury, Massachusetts

A Psalm of Life

DVD, Track 21

> *Life that shall send*
> *A challenge to its end,*
> *And when it comes, say, "Welcome, friend."*

WHAT THE HEART OF THE YOUNG
MAN SAID TO THE PSALMIST

Tell me not, in mournful numbers,
    Life is but an empty dream!
For the soul is dead that slumbers,
    And things are not what they seem.

Life is real—life is earnest—
    And the grave is not its goal:
Dust thou art, to dust returnest,
    Was not spoken of the soul.

Not enjoyment, and not sorrow,
    Is our destined end or way;

But to *act*, that each to-morrow
   Find us farther than to-day.

Art is long, and time is fleeting,
   And our hearts, though stout and brave,
Still, like muffled drums, are beating
   Funeral marches to the grave.

In the world's broad field of battle,
   In the bivouac of Life,
Be not like dumb, driven cattle!
   Be a hero in the strife!

Trust no Future, howe'er pleasant!
   Let the dead Past bury its dead!
Act—act in the glorious Present!
   Heart within, and God o'er head!

Lives of great men all remind us
   We can make *our* lives sublime,
And, departing, leave behind us
   Footsteps on the sands of time.

Footsteps, that, perhaps another,
   Sailing o'er life's solemn main,
A forlorn and shipwrecked brother,
   Seeing, shall take heart again.

Let us then be up and doing,
   With a heart for any fate;
Still achieving, still pursuing,
   Learn to labor and to wait.

RICHARD LOVELACE

ENGLAND · 1618–1657

This is a rather antique poem. I confess the first three stanzas sound almost as though they come from a historical romantic novel. But the last stanza is transcendent, speaking to any gender, any time, and with a spirituality that curiously contradicts the previous stanzas.

—Carolyn Ferrucci, 54, Health Care Consultant, Natick, Massachusetts

To Althea, from Prison

When Love with unconfinèd wings
Hovers within my gates,
And my divine Althea brings
To whisper at the grates;
When I lie tangled in her hair
And fettered to her eye,
The gods that wanton in the air
Know no such liberty.

When flowing cups run swiftly round,
With no allaying Thames,
Our careless heads with roses bound,
Our hearts with loyal flames;
When thirsty grief in wine we steep,
When healths and draughts go free,
Fishes, that tipple in the deep,
Know no such liberty.

When, like committed linnets, I
With shriller throat shall sing
The sweetness, mercy, majesty,
And glories of my King;
When I shall voice aloud how good
He is, how great should be,
Enlargèd winds, that curl the flood,
Know no such liberty.

Stone walls do not a prison make,
Nor iron bars a cage;

Minds innocent and quiet take
That for an hermitage.
If I have freedom in my love,
And in my soul am free,
Angels alone, that soar above,
Enjoy such liberty.

ROBERT LOWELL

UNITED STATES • 1917–1977

When I first studied Lowell's poems in school, I was drawn to his personal voice and his focus on family and U.S. history. His pacifism impressed me; I had just returned from Vietnam and had joined Vietnam Veterans Against the War and the Martin Luther King Social Action Council. This poem is set on Marlborough Street, where I used to walk as a child on visits to the dentist. It's possible Lowell was living there at the time, and that I passed his door.

—Peter Nicoletta, 54, Teacher, Freeland, Washington

Memories of West Street and Lepke

Only teaching on Tuesdays, book-worming
in pajamas fresh from the washer each morning,
I hog a whole house on Boston's
"hardly passionate Marlborough Street,"
where even the man
scavenging filth in the back alley trash cans,
has two children, a beach wagon, a helpmate,
and is a "young Republican."
I have a nine months' daughter,
young enough to be my granddaughter.
Like the sun she rises in her flame-flamingo infants' wear.

These are the tranquillized *Fifties,*
and I am forty. Ought I to regret my seedtime?
I was a fire-breathing Catholic C.O.,
and made my manic statement,
telling off the state and president, and then
sat waiting sentence in the bull pen
beside a Negro boy with curlicues
of marijuana in his hair.

Given a year,
I walked on the roof of the West Street Jail, a short
enclosure like my school soccer court,
and saw the Hudson River once a day

through sooty clothesline entanglements
and bleaching khaki tenements.
Strolling, I yammered metaphysics with Abramowitz,
a jaundice-yellow ("it's really tan")
and fly-weight pacifist,
so vegetarian,
he wore rope shoes and preferred fallen fruit.
He tried to convert Bioff and Brown,
the Hollywood pimps, to his diet.
Hairy, muscular, suburban,
wearing chocolate double-breasted suits,
they blew their tops and beat him black and blue.

I was so out of things, I'd never heard
of the Jehovah's Witnesses.
"Are you a C.O.?" I asked a fellow jailbird.
"No," he answered, "I'm a J.W."
He taught me the "hospital tuck,"
and pointed out the T-shirted back
of *Murder Incorporated's* Czar Lepke,
there piling towels on a rack,
or dawdling off to his little segregated cell full
of things forbidden the common man:
a portable radio, a dresser, two toy American
flags tied together with a ribbon of Easter palm.
Flabby, bald, lobotomized,
he drifted in a sheepish calm,
where no agonizing reappraisal
jarred his concentration on the electric chair—
hanging like an oasis in his air
of lost connections. . . .

Robert Lowell   157

It's beautiful. It reminds me now of a place and of some moments; but when I first read it I loved how it seemed distant but warm, sad but not unsatisfied; and the quiet of the close watching, the snowplow coming up the hill.
—David Cole, 48, Advertising Professional, Miami, Florida

The Old Flame

My old flame, my wife!
Remember our lists of birds?
One morning last summer, I drove
by our house in Maine. It was still
on top of its hill—

Now a red ear of Indian maize
was splashed on the door.
Old Glory with thirteen stars
hung on a pole. The clapboard
was old-red schoolhouse red.

Inside, a new landlord,
a new wife, a new broom!
Atlantic seaboard antique shop
pewter and plunder
shone in each room.

A new frontier!
No running next door
now to phone the sheriff
for his taxi to Bath
and the State Liquor Store!

No one saw your ghostly
imaginary lover
stare through the window,
and tighten
the scarf at his throat.

Health to the new people,
health to their flag, to their old
restored house on the hill!

Robert Lowell

Everything had been swept bare,
furnished, garnished, and aired.

Everything's changed for the best—
how quivering and fierce we were,
there snowbound together,
simmering like wasps
in our tent of books!

Poor ghost, old love, speak
with your old voice
of flaming insight
that kept us awake all night.
In one bed and apart,

we heard the plow
groaning up hill—
a red light, then a blue,
as it tossed off the snow
to the side of the road.

Robert Lowell

ANTONIO MACHADO

SPAIN • 1875–1939

My father-in-law was born in Spain into a working-class family. The youngest of five, he left home at the age of nineteen to fight in the Spanish Civil War, on the side of the Republican Army. He ended the war in a concentration camp in France, and in 1939, while a prisoner of war, he was given the opportunity to emigrate to Mexico. Alone, and barely twenty-one, he joined a large wave of refugees seeking political asylum that left Spain forever on ships bound for Mexico, or Argentina, or Cuba. A largely self-educated man, he had a great love of literature and poetry. He often jokingly threatened to retire to a cell in a monastery, with only the works of Cervantes, Walt Whitman, Miguel Hernandez, and Antonio Machado for company. This was the poem that he would frequently recite to his grandchildren, and anyone else who would care to stop and listen. It reminds me of his love for the Spain he had to leave behind, and the essence of this individual who always strove just to be a good man.

—Vivian Serrano Villaseñor, 52, Librarian, Arlington, Virginia

Portrait

My childhood is memories of a patio in Seville,
and a garden where sunlit lemons are growing yellow;
my youth twenty years on the earth of Castile;
what I lived a few things you'll forgive me for omitting.

A great seducer I was not, nor the lover of Juliet;
—the oafish way I dress is enough to say that—
but the arrow Cupid planned for me I got,
and I loved whenever women found a home in me.

A flow of leftist blood moves through my body,
but my poems rise from a calm and deep spring.
There is a man of rule who behaves as he should, but more
than him, I am, in the good sense of the word, good.

I adore beauty, and following contemporary thought
have cut some old roses from the garden of Ronsard;

but the new lotions and feathers are not for me;
I am not one of the blue jays who sing so well.

I dislike hollow tenors who warble of love,
and the chorus of crickets singing to the moon.
I fall silent so as to separate voices from echoes,
and I listen among the voices to one voice and only one.

Am I classic or Romantic? Who knows. I want to leave
my poetry as a fighter leaves his sword, known
for the masculine hand that closed around it,
not for the coded mark of the proud forger.

I talk always to the man who walks along with me;
—men who talk to themselves hope to talk to God someday—
My soliloquies amount to discussions with this friend,
who taught me the secret of loving human beings.

In the end, I owe you nothing; you owe me what I've written.
I turn to my work; with what I've earned I pay
for my clothes and hat, the house in which I live,
the food that feeds my body, the bed on which I sleep.

And when the day arrives for the last leaving of all,
and the ship that never returns to port is ready to go,
you'll find me on board, light, with few belongings,
almost naked like the children of the sea.

Translated from the Spanish by Robert Bly

ARCHIBALD MACLEISH

UNITED STATES · 1892–1982

Rereadable.
—David Webb, 58, Retired, Lynchburg, Virginia

Ars Poetica

A poem should be palpable and mute
As a globed fruit,

Dumb
As old medallions to the thumb,

Silent as the sleeve-worn stone
Of casement ledges where the moss has grown—

A poem should be wordless
As the flight of birds.

       *

A poem should be motionless in time
As the moon climbs,

Leaving, as the moon releases
Twig by twig the night-entangled trees,

Leaving, as the moon behind the winter leaves,
Memory by memory the mind—

A poem should be motionless in time
As the moon climbs.

       *

A poem should be equal to:
Not true.

For all the history of grief
An empty doorway and a maple leaf.

For love
The leaning grasses and two lights above the sea—

A poem should not mean
But be.

HEATHER MCHUGH

UNITED STATES • B. 1948

I love this poem because it can't be translated, so to me it feels intensely private and ingenious. There's a great mix of anger, fierceness, and longing, and the language innovates around the usual terms for desire. The poem feels careful to me, so aware of how thin a line there always is between the expression of love and the loss of power such expression suffers when it fails to take a risk.

—Jennifer Boyden, 32, Teacher/Writer, Walla Walla, Washington

Language Lesson 1976

When Americans say a man
takes liberties, they mean

he's gone too far. In Philadelphia today I saw
a kid on a leash look mom-ward

and announce his fondest wish: one
bicentennial burger, hold

the relish. Hold is forget,
in American.

On the courts of Philadelphia
the rich prepare

to serve, to fault. The language is a game as well,
in which love can mean nothing,

doubletalk mean lie. I'm saying
doubletalk with me. I'm saying

go so far the customs are untold.
Make nothing without words,

and let me be
the one you never hold.

James Merrill

UNITED STATES • 1926–1995

This poem appeared in the New Yorker *the week my husband left me. There was no warning. In my shock, I felt I was there, fallen into a mad scene, a scene that began in such splendid perfection, and ended in a burst of grief. All the more poignant because I'd realized, and grown to love, that the evolution of the relationship was in the comforts of the routine of living together, and seeing it through to the end. I was enraged about losing that. The poem still haunts me.*

—Amber Wong, 43, Environmental Engineer, Seattle, Washington

The Mad Scene

Again last night I dreamed the dream called Laundry.
In it, the sheets and towels of a life we were going to share,
The milk-stiff bibs, the shroud, each rag to be ever
Trampled or soiled, bled on or groped for blindly,
Came swooning out of an enormous willow hamper
Onto moon-marbly boards. We had just met. I watched
From outer darkness. I had dressed myself in clothes
Of a new fiber that never stains or wrinkles, never
Wears thin. The opera house sparkled with tiers
And tiers of eyes, like mine enlarged by belladonna,
Trained inward. There I saw the cloud-clot, gust by gust,
Form, and the lightning bite, and the roan mane unloosen.
Fingers were running in panic over the flute's nine gates.
Why did I flinch? I loved you. And in the downpour laughed
To have us wrung white, gnarled together, one
Topmost mordent of wisteria,
As the lean tree burst into grief.

W. S. MERWIN

UNITED STATES · B. 1927

*A reading reveals its great musicality: implicit in this wonderful work are
the songs of the whales as well as American blues music.*

—Gloria Jaguden, 70, Retired, Los Angeles, California

The Shore

How can anyone know that a whale
two hundred years ago could hear another
whale at the opposite end of the earth
or tell how long the eyes
of a whale have faced both halves of the world
and have found light far down in old company

with the sounds of hollow iron charging
clanging through the oceans and with the circuitries
and the harpoons of humans
and the poisoning of the seas
a whale can hear no farther through the present
than a jet can fly in a few minutes

in the days of their hearing the great Blues gathered like clouds
the sunlight under the sea's surfaces sank
into their backs as into the water around them
through which they flew invisible from above
except as flashes of movement
and they could hear each other's voices wherever they went

once it is on its own a Blue can wander
the whole world beholding both sides of the water
raising in each ocean the songs of the Blues
that it learned from distances it can no longer hear
it can fly all its life without ever meeting another Blue
this is what we are doing this is the way we sing oh Blue Blue

EDNA ST. VINCENT MILLAY

UNITED STATES · 1892–1950

I first came across this poem when I was an intense, flute-playing teenager in 1966. My girlfriends and I all played the flute, followed flute players around New York City and talked a lot about depression. Besides expressing my feelings for me, at a time when I was still unaware or unable to do so myself, Millay's poem awakened my sense of the connections between music and poetry. I lost track of the poem for several years as I married, bore children, studied, only to come across it again on my seventy-year-old mother's refrigerator door. I had found an old friend. My feelings about my life have changed, but not my feelings about Millay's poem.

—Judith Everitt, 53, Elementary School Librarian, Skillman, New Jersey

On Hearing a Symphony of Beethoven

Sweet sounds, oh, beautiful music, do not cease!
Reject me not into the world again.
With you alone is excellence and peace,
Mankind made plausible, his purpose plain.
Enchanted in your air benign and shrewd,
With limbs a-sprawl and empty faces pale,
The spiteful and the stingy and the rude
Sleep like the scullions in the fairy-tale.
This moment is the best the world can give:
The tranquil blossom on the tortured stem.
Reject me not, sweet sounds! oh, let me live,
Till Doom espy my towers and scatter them,
A city spell-bound under the aging sun,
Music my rampart, and my only one.

When I was a teenager, I took this poem as ideal romance. Then, forty-five years later, "Recuerdo" appeared on the New York City subways I rode with my grandson when he was two. He loved the poem as soon as I read it to him, and he knew it by heart then. Then I realized that the music brings the poem close.

—Madeline Tiger, 64, Teacher, Upper Montclair, New Jersey

I have not lived in Manhattan for thirty-three years and this poem indulges the hubris: Staten Island ferry, youth, craziness, love, apples and pears, the wind coming cold and the sun dripping gold.

—Paula Boyer Rougny, 64, Editor/Writer, Bangor, Maine

Recuerdo

We were very tired, we were very merry—
We had gone back and forth all night on the ferry.
It was bare and bright, and smelled like a stable—
But we looked into a fire, we leaned across a table,
We lay on a hill-top underneath the moon;
And the whistles kept blowing, and the dawn came soon.

We were very tired, we were very merry—
We had gone back and forth all night on the ferry;
And you ate an apple, and I ate a pear,
From a dozen of each we had bought somewhere;
And the sky went wan, and the wind came cold,
And the sun rose dripping, a bucketful of gold.

We were very tired, we were very merry,
We had gone back and forth all night on the ferry.
We hailed, "Good morrow, mother!" to a shawl-covered head,
And bought a morning paper, which neither of us read;
And she wept, "God bless you!" for the apples and pears,
And we gave her all our money but our subway fares.

Edna St. Vincent Millay   167

Czeslaw Milosz

POLAND · B. 1911

The poem is better than a jury verdict, more ruthless than an execution, yet is compassionate to its core.

—Peggy Little, 44, Attorney, Stratford, Connecticut

You Who Wronged

You who wronged a simple man
Bursting into laughter at the crime,
And kept a pack of fools around you
To mix good and evil, to blur the line,

Though everyone bowed down before you,
Saying virtue and wisdom lit your way,
Striking gold medals in your honor,
Glad to have survived another day,

Do not feel safe. The poet remembers.
You can kill one, but another is born.
The words are written down, the deed, the date.

And you'd have done better with a winter dawn,
A rope, and a branch bowed beneath your weight.

Translated from the Polish by Richard Lourie

John Milton

ENGLAND · 1608–1674

Now that I've reached the age of ninety and am not exactly in the pink of health, this is my favorite poem. I repeat it to myself many times, day and night. If Milton and Beethoven could contribute so much to humanity despite their handicaps, the rest of us should really count our blessings.
—Dinah Wolfe, 90, Richmond, Virginia

When I consider how my light is spent

When I consider how my light is spent
Ere half my days in this dark world and wide,
And that one Talent which is death to hide
Lodged with me useless, though my soul more bent
To serve therewith my Maker, and present
My true account, lest He returning chide,
"Doth God exact day-labour, light denied?"
I fondly ask. But Patience, to prevent
That murmur, soon replies, "God doth not need
Either man's work or his own gifts. Who best
Bear his mild yoke, they serve him best. His state
Is kingly: thousands at his bidding speed,
And post o'er land and ocean without rest;
They also serve who only stand and wait."

GABRIELA MISTRAL

CHILE • 1889–1957

To work with the children, for me, is my mission. I see that other children don't have the love that I received in my family, and I want to give this love to them—that they feel they are the only thing that I have in this world. They ask me, "Christina why are you here?" And I say, "Because you are here. The only reason for me is you are here."

—Sister Maria Christina Sanchez Escobar, 56, Social Worker,
    Milbrook, New York

Piececitos

DVD, Track 19

Little feet of children
blue with cold,
how can they see you and not cover you—
dear God!

Little wounded feet
cut by every stone,
hurt by snow
and mire.

Man, blind, does not know
that where you pass,
you leave a flower
of living light.

And where you set
your little bleeding foot,
the spikenard blooms
more fragrant.

Walking straight paths,
be heroic, little feet,
as you are
perfect.

Little feet of children,
two tiny suffering jewels,
how can people pass
and not see you!

Translated from the Spanish by Doris Dana

MARIANNE MOORE

UNITED STATES • 1887–1972

In a few short lines, Marianne Moore has written a poem that actually feels gelatinous. It moves like a jellyfish. I get the image of the "moon jellies" in a fish tank at Brookfield Zoo swimming around and always think of this poem when I watch them.
—Keith Lewis, 32, Teacher, Lisle, Illinois

A Jellyfish

Visible, invisible,
　　a fluctuating charm
an amber-tinctured amethyst
　　inhabits it, your arm
approaches and it opens
　　and it closes; you had meant
to catch it and it quivers;
　　you abandon your intent.

What Are Years?

What is our innocence,
what is our guilt? All are
    naked, none is safe. And whence
is courage: the unanswered question,
the resolute doubt,—
dumbly calling, deafly listening—that
in misfortune, even death,
        encourages others
        and in its defeat, stirs

                the soul to be strong? He
sees deep and is glad, who
    accedes to mortality
and in his imprisonment rises
upon himself as
the sea in a chasm, struggling to be
free and unable to be,
        in its surrendering
        finds its continuing.

So he who strongly feels,
behaves. The very bird,
    grown taller as he sings, steels
his form straight up. Though he is captive,
his mighty singing
says, satisfaction is a lowly
thing, how pure a thing is joy.
        This is mortality,
        this is eternity.

THOMAS MOORE

IRELAND · 1779–1852

My favorite pastime is to go camping with family and friends, spending long hours around a campfire while sharing food, drink, and ourselves. A favorite place of ours, twelve years running, is next to the stream at Lost Mine Campground in the mountains of Nantahala National Forest in western North Carolina. This poem sparks the same feelings of love and friendship I experience during our camping trips. One of my children will read it at my funeral.

—J. M. M. Harrison, 54, Chemical Engineer, Atlanta, Georgia

The Meeting of the Waters

There is not in the wide world a valley so sweet
As that vale in whose bosom the bright waters meet;
Oh! the last rays of feeling and life must depart,
Ere the bloom of that valley shall fade from my heart.

Yet it *was* not that nature had shed o'er the scene
Her purest of crystal and brightest of green;
'Twas *not* her soft magic of streamlet or hill,
Oh! no,—it was something more exquisite still.

'Twas that friends, the belov'd of my bosom, were near,
Who made every dear scene of enchantment more dear,
And who felt how the best charms of nature improve,
When we see them reflected from looks that we love.

Sweet vale of Avoca! how calm could I rest
In thy bosom of shade, with the friends I love best,
Where the storms that we feel in this cold world should cease,
And our hearts, like thy waters, be mingled in peace.

Howard Nemerov

UNITED STATES • 1920–1991

I love the simplicity of this poem and its beautiful knitting together of child-hood and age, of first things and last things, and its poignant soft surprise in the final line. I also rejoice to see poets, century after century, using the sonnet in fresh and wonderful ways.
—Ralph Birdsey, 62, Investment Manager, Atlanta, Georgia

The Snow Globe

A long time ago, when I was a child,
They left my light on while I went to sleep,
As though they would have wanted me beguiled
By brightness if at all; dark was too deep.

And they left me one toy, a village white
With the fresh snow and silently in glass
Frozen forever. But if you shook it,
The snow would rise up in the rounded space

And from the limits of the universe
Snow itself down again. O world of white,
First home of dreams! Now that I have my dead,
I want so cold an emblem to rehearse
How many of them have gone from the world's light,
As I have gone, too, from my snowy bed.

Pablo Neruda

CHILE • 1904–1973

My husband was killed at the age of thirty-one. The restlessness of Joaquín, even after death, expressed the very nature of my late husband, Ricardo. This poem seems to have been written about him. I lost him over sixteen years ago, but this poem still brings him back to me.

—Liz Melara, 42, Community Relations Representative, Oak Park, Illinois

Absence of Joaquín

From now on, like a departure seen from a distance,
in funeral positions of smoke or solitary embankments,
from now on I see him hurtling into his death
and behind him I hear the days of time closing.

From now on, with a jolt, I hear him going,
rushing on in the waters, in certain waters, in one particular
    ocean,
and then, when he strikes, drops rise, and a noise,
a resolute muffled noise, I hear it forming,
a stroke of water lashed by his weight,
and from somewhere, from somewhere I hear those waters tossing
    and splashing
and they splash over me, those waters, and burn like acids.

His apparel of dreams and immoderate nights,
his disobedient soul, his prepared pallor
sleep with him once and for all, and he sleeps,
for his passion plummeted into the sea of the dead,
sinking violently, joining it coldly.

Translated from the Spanish by W. S. Merwin

LORINE NIEDECKER

UNITED STATES • 1903–1970

When I was living in California in the late 1980s and going through a
divorce my grandmother died. I longed to be in Wisconsin with my family.
I started to look through some books of poetry by Lorine Niedecker and felt
like I was transported there. Her poetry helped me deal with my grief. Later,
nearly two years ago, my father died. I was back in Wisconsin by then. The
grief threatened to drown me. I reached for my Niedecker books. I knew
my father loved me but didn't understand me. There was a gulf between us.
I feel that Lorine Niedecker summed up this aspect of the father-
daughter relationship wonderfully in her spare, beautiful poem.

—Amy Mussell, 39, Sheboygan, Wisconsin

He lived—childhood summers

He lived—childhood summers
      thru bare feet
then years of money's lack
      and heat

beside the river—out of flood
      came his wood, dog
woman, lost her, daughter—
      prologue

to planting trees. He buried carp
      beneath the rose
where grass-still
      the marsh rail goes.

To bankers on high land
      he opened his wine tank.
He wished his only daughter
      to work in the bank

but he'd given her a source
      to sustain her—
a weedy speech,
      a marshy retainer.

FRANK O'HARA

UNITED STATES • 1926–1966

I'm a lifelong inveterate fan of jazz and an unapologetic Beatnik. This poem is evocative of the time, the place, the ambiance.
—Dolly Spalding, 60, Editor, Flagstaff, Arizona

The Day Lady Died

It is 12:20 in New York a Friday
three days after Bastille day, yes
it is 1959 and I go get a shoeshine
because I will get off the 4:19 in Easthampton
at 7:15 and then go straight to dinner
and I don't know the people who will feed me

I walk up the muggy street beginning to sun
and have a hamburger and a malted and buy
an ugly NEW WORLD WRITING to see what the poets
in Ghana are doing these days
                                        I go on to the bank
and Miss Stillwagon (first name Linda I once heard)
doesn't even look up my balance for once in her life
and in the GOLDEN GRIFFIN I get a little Verlaine
for Patsy with drawings by Bonnard although I do
think of Hesiod, trans. Richmond Lattimore or
Brendan Behan's new play or *Le Balcon* or *Les Nègres*
of Genet, but I don't, I stick with Verlaine
after practically going to sleep with quandariness

and for Mike I just stroll into the PARK LANE
Liquor Store and ask for a bottle of Strega and
then I go back where I came from to 6th Avenue
and the tobacconist in the Ziegfeld Theatre and
casually ask for a carton of Gauloises and a carton
of Picayunes, and a NEW YORK POST with her face on it

and I am sweating a lot by now and thinking of
leaning on the john door in the 5 SPOT
while she whispered a song along the keyboard
to Mal Waldron and everyone and I stopped breathing

I first encountered this poem in college in a poetry appreciation class. In college, most people feel that their life is a little bit out of control—and the voice in this poem is someone who is very definitely out of control. There's a lot of poetry that talks about how stable and wonderful life is, and "the flowers are blooming." This poem is from the opposite end of that spectrum. I think that appealed to me as a college student facing the future and not sure whether I was going to be racing, like the poet, or going into the garden, as it were.

—Richard Samuel, 48, Glassblower, Seattle, Washington

Poem

DVD, Track 6

Lana Turner has collapsed!
I was trotting along and suddenly
it started raining and snowing
and you said it was hailing
but hailing hits you on the head
hard so it was really snowing and
raining and I was in such a hurry
to meet you but the traffic
was acting exactly like the sky
and suddenly I see a headline
LANA TURNER HAS COLLAPSED!
there is no snow in Hollywood
there is no rain in California
I have been to lots of parties
and acted perfectly disgraceful
but I never actually collapsed
oh Lana Turner we love you get up

Frank O'Hara

179

I've been carrying this poem around in my wallet for about seven years. I refer to it all the time. I like how it immediately sounds like a sad poem, but after reflection, it communicates such a positive idea.

—Tom Llewellyn, 33, Advertising Writer

Poem

"Two communities outside Birmingham, Alabama, are still searching for their dead."—News Telecast

And tomorrow morning at 8 o'clock in Springfield, Massachusetts,
my oldest aunt will be buried from a convent.
Spring is here and I am staying here, I'm not going.
Do birds fly? I am thinking my own thoughts, who else's?

    When I die, don't come, I wouldn't want a leaf
    to turn away from the sun—it loves it there.
    There's nothing so spiritual about being happy
    but you can't miss a day of it, because it doesn't last.

So this is the devil's dance? Well I was born to dance.
It's a sacred duty, like being in love with an ape,
and eventually I'll reach some great conclusion, like assumption,
when at last I meet exhaustion in these flowers, go straight up.

Frank O'Hara

GEORGE OPPEN

UNITED STATES • 1908–1984

I grew up in Northern California—in fact, I am of the fifth generation of my family to do so—and the image of the summer fog, so elusive yet tangible, touches my sensibilities.

—Sharon Coleman, 32, Graduate Student, San Mateo, California

This seems to me one of the very few love poems of our time that extends our knowledge of love itself.

—Theodore Enslin, 74, Writer, Milbridge, Maine

The Forms of Love

Parked in the fields
All night
So many years ago,
We saw
A lake beside us
When the moon rose.
I remember

Leaving that ancient car
Together. I remember
Standing in the white grass
Beside it. We groped
Our way together
Downhill in the bright
Incredible light

Beginning to wonder
Whether it could be lake
Or fog
We saw, our heads
Ringing under the stars we walked
To where it would have wet our feet
Had it been water

It's a reaffirmation of the mysteries we often take for granted, or choose not to see.

—Salvatore Safina, 37, College Instructor, Oak Creek, Wisconsin

Psalm

Veritas sequitur . . .

In the small beauty of the forest
The wild deer bedding down—
That they are there

               Their eyes
Effortless, the soft lips
Nuzzle and the alien small teeth
Tear at the grass

               The roots of it
Dangle from their mouths
Scattering earth in the strange woods.
They who are there.

               Their paths
Nibbled thru the fields, the leaves that shade them
Hang in the distances
Of sun

               The small nouns
Crying faith
In this in which the wild deer
Startle, and stare out.

George Oppen

WILFRED OWEN

ENGLAND · 1893–1918

When I was about twelve years old, in seventh grade, my seventh grade teacher gave us this poem as an assignment. A lot of the kids in the class found it to be kind of funny—you know at that age they read things and they don't understand how serious they are. But the way things were in my family—my father was blinded during World War II—this poem really brought home to me the tragedies that occur during war and things that had happened in my father's life that I wasn't even aware of.

—Mary McWhorter, 39, Accountant, Stockton, California

Dulce Et Decorum Est   DVD, Track 20

Bent double, like old beggars under sacks,
Knock-kneed, coughing like hags, we cursed through sludge,
Till on the haunting flares we turned our backs
And towards our distant rest began to trudge.
Men marched asleep. Many had lost their boots
But limped on, blood-shod. All went lame; all blind;
Drunk with fatigue; deaf even to the hoots
Of tired, outstripped Five-Nines that dropped behind.

Gas! GAS! Quick, boys—An ecstasy of fumbling,
Fitting the clumsy helmets just in time;
But someone still was yelling out and stumbling
And flound'ring like a man in fire or lime . . .
Dim, through the misty panes and thick green light,
As under a green sea, I saw him drowning.

In all my dreams, before my helpless sight,
He plunges at me, guttering, choking, drowning.

If in some smothering dreams you too could pace
Behind the wagon that we flung him in,
And watch the white eyes writhing in his face,
His hanging face, like a devil's sick of sin;
If you could hear, at every jolt, the blood
Come gargling from the froth-corrupted lungs,
Obscene as cancer, bitter as the cud

Of vile, incurable sores on innocent tongues,—
My friend, you would not tell with such high zest
To children ardent for some desperate glory,
The old Lie: Dulce et decorum est
Pro patria mori.

Wilfred Owen

KENNETH PATCHEN

UNITED STATES • 1911–1972

It speaks in the spaces between the noises of our noisy world.
—Ruth Gordon, 66, Retired Librarian, Cloverdale, California

At the New Year

In the shape of this night, in the still fall
    of snow, Father
In all that is cold and tiny, these little birds
    and children
In everything that moves tonight, the trolleys
    and the lovers, Father
In the great hush of country, in the ugly noise
    of our cities
In this deep throw of stars, in those trenches
    where the dead are, Father
In all the wide land waiting, and in the liners
    out on the black water
In all that has been said bravely, in all that is
    mean anywhere in the world, Father
In all that is good and lovely, in every house
    where sham and hatred are
In the name of those who wait, in the sound
    of angry voices, Father
Before the bells ring, before this little point in time
    has rushed us on
Before this clean moment has gone, before this night
    turns to face tomorrow, Father
There is this high singing in the air
Forever this sorrowful human face in eternity's window
And there are other bells that we would ring, Father
Other bells that we would ring.

OCTAVIO PAZ

MEXICO • 1914–1998

When I was thirty-eight and my daughter was born it was a cold and stormy winter. She was born in January. I had just gone back to work in March and we had never gone out at night and left her with a babysitter. Our first night out together—April 15, 1993—was spent listening to Octavio Paz read his poetry. I remember sitting in a church across the street from the Folger Library in Washington. I was thinking of all the possible catastrophes that could be occurring at home. He read "Dawn" and all of my focus turned to him.

—Deborah Burke, 44, Radiologist, Rockville, Maryland

Dawn

Cold rapid hands
draw back one by one
the bandages of dark
I open my eyes
    still
I am living
   at the center
of a wound still fresh

Translated from the Spanish by Charles Tomlinson

Its simple, comprehensible words contain a profound truth, which reveals the rule of nature, even to human beings. I learn from this poem that everything can't live in isolation and is affected by others.
—Ai H. Szeto, 22, Student, Miami, Florida

Wind and Water and Stone

For Roger Caillois

The water hollowed the stone,
the wind dispersed the water,
the stone stopped the wind.
Water and wind and stone.

The wind sculpted the stone,
the stone is a cup of water,
the water runs off and is wind.
Stone and wind and water.

The wind sings in its turnings,
the water murmurs as it goes,
the motionless stone is quiet.
Wind and water and stone.

One is the other, and is neither:
among their empty names
they pass and disappear,
water and stone and wind.

Translated from the Spanish by Mark Strand

Fernando Pessoa

PORTUGAL • 1888–1935

*I don't remember where I first read this poem, but it took on great signifi-
cance when my first husband Michael became terminally ill with cancer at
age thirty-four. The sonnet spoke to me in a way nothing else did at the
time.*

—Justine Strand, 47, Physician Assistant, Durham, North Carolina

When in the widening circle of rebirth

When in the widening circle of rebirth
To a new flesh my traveled soul shall come,
And try again the unremembered earth
With the old sadness for the immortal home,
Shall I revisit these same differing fields
And cull the old new flowers with the same sense,
That some small breath of foiled remembrance yields,
Of more age than my days in this pretence?
Shall I again regret strange faces lost
Of which the present memory is forgot
And but in unseen bulks of vagueness tossed
Out of the closed sea and black night of Thought?
Were thy face one, what sweetness will't not be,
Though by blind feeling, to remember thee!

SYLVIA PLATH

UNITED STATES • 1932–1963

It was a date situation. I had wanted to go out with this girl and I just ended up feeling very bad at the end of it. It just didn't work out the way I wanted it to. I ended up feeling kind of lonely and . . . "bereft," I suppose. I came home and I opened this book and I read some of the poems. Up until that point I think my sense of poetry is that it was a sort of grandiose, highfalutin, not very real way of using language. And I looked at this stuff and I could not believe it. It was light-years beyond anything else I had ever read. It was powerful, it was rough, it was bitter, it was caustic. It was, at the same time, really urgent about a need for love.

—Seph Rodney, 28, Photographer, Santa Monica, California

Nick and the Candlestick

DVD, Track 9

I am a miner. The light burns blue.
Waxy stalactites
Drip and thicken, tears

The earthen womb
Exudes from its dead boredom.
Black bat airs

Wrap me, raggy shawls,
Cold homicides.
They weld to me like plums.

Old cave of calcium
Icicles, old echoer.
Even the newts are white,

Those holy Joes.
And the fish, the fish—
Christ! They are panes of ice,

A vice of knives,
A piranha
Religion, drinking

Its first communion out of my live toes.
The candle
Gulps and recovers its small altitude,

Its yellows hearten.
O love, how did you get here?
O embryo

Remembering, even in sleep,
Your crossed position.
The blood blooms clean

In you, ruby.
The pain
You wake to is not yours.

Love, love,
I have hung our cave with roses.
With soft rugs—

The last of Victoriana.
Let the stars
Plummet to their dark address,

Let the mercuric
Atoms that cripple drip
Into the terrible well,

You are the one
Solid the spaces lean on, envious.
You are the baby in the barn.

EDGAR ALLAN POE

UNITED STATES • 1809–1849

It is a lot like everyday life. This is a poem for anybody who has ever felt out of place.

—Joseph Anterola, 13, Student, Rockwell, North Carolina

Alone

From childhood's hour I have not been
As others were—I have not seen
As others saw—I could not bring
My passions from a common spring—
From the same source I have not taken
My sorrow—I could not awaken
My heart to joy at the same tone—
And all I loved—*I* loved alone.
Then—in my childhood—in the dawn
Of a most stormy life—was drawn
From ev'ry depth of good and ill
The mystery which binds me still—
From the torrent, or the fountain—
From the red cliff of the mountain—
From the sun that round me rolled
In its autumn tint of gold—
From the lightning in the sky
As it passed me flying by—
From the thunder, and the storm—
And the cloud that took the form
(When the rest of Heaven was blue)
Of a demon in my view.

EZRA POUND

UNITED STATES • 1885–1972

Since the day I first read this poem it has become part of my life. I appreciate every hour for what it is. Nothing more, nothing less.
—Kathy Young, 48, Homemaker, Toms River, New Jersey

Erat Hora

"Thank you, whatever comes." And then she turned
And, as the ray of sun on hanging flowers
Fades when the wind hath lifted them aside,
Went swiftly from me. Nay, whatever comes
One hour was sunlit and the most high gods
May not make boast of any better thing
Than to have watched that hour as it passed.

I have a dog. Sometimes when she's in the backyard she suddenly, with no stimulus apparent to me, becomes very agitated and runs off into the bushes by the fence wandering about doing some "dog" thing, which seems the most important thing in the world to her, but I cannot fathom the reasons. It reminds me of the actions of business managers, government officials, personal acquaintances, drivers on the freeway, members of committees, and so on, who become obsessed with an endless succession of near-term objectives to the neglect of other people and even their own long-term interests. Curious habits indeed.
—Bill Molander, U.S.A.

Meditatio

When I carefully consider the curious habits of dogs
I am compelled to conclude
That man is the superior animal.

When I consider the curious habits of man
I confess, my friend, I am puzzled.

ADRIENNE RICH

UNITED STATES • B. 1929

The poem speaks to the need for perseverance. It also honors the human mind for having that perseverance.
—Judith Chelte, 51, Teacher, Chicopee, Massachusetts

The Diamond Cutters

However legendary,
The stone is still a stone,
Though it had once resisted
The weight of Africa,
The hammer-blows of time
That wear to bits of rubble
The mountain and the pebble—
But not this coldest one.

Now, you intelligence
So late dredged up from dark
Upon whose smoky walls
Bison took fumbling form
Or flint was edged on flint—
Now, careful arriviste,
Delineate at will
Incisions in the ice.

Be serious, because
The stone may have contempt
For too-familiar hands,
And because all you do
Loses or gains by this:
Respect the adversary,
Meet it with tools refined,
And thereby set your price.

Be hard of heart, because
The stone must leave your hand.
Although you liberate
Pure and expensive fires

Fit to enamor Shebas,
Keep your desire apart.
Love only what you do,
And not what you have done.

Be proud, when you have set
The final spoke of flame
In that prismatic wheel,
And nothing's left this day
Except to see the sun
Shine on the false and the true,
And know that Africa
Will yield you more to do.

It is one that I reread every so often over the years, and now in middle age I still find it moving and meaningful.
—Charlene Duroni, U.S.A.

Phantasia for Elvira Shatayev

> *Leader of a women's climbing team, all of whom
> died in a storm on Lenin Peak, August 1974.
> Later, Shatayev's husband found and buried the bodies.*

The cold felt cold until our blood
grew colder   then the wind
died down and we slept

If in this sleep I speak
it's with a voice no longer personal
(I want to say   *with voices*)
When the wind tore   our breath from us at last
we had no need of words
For months   for years   each one of us
had felt her own *yes* growing in her
slowly forming   as she stood at windows   waited
for trains   mended her rucksack   combed her hair
What we were to learn   was simply   what we had
up here   as out of all words   that *yes* gathered

its forces   fused itself   and only just in time
to meet a *No* of no degrees
the black hole   sucking the world in

I feel you climbing toward me
your cleated bootsoles leaving   their geometric bite
colossally embossed   on microscopic crystals
as when I trailed you in the Caucasus
Now I am further
ahead   than either of us dreamed   anyone would be
I have become
the white snow packed like asphalt by the wind
the women I love   lightly flung   against the mountain
that blue sky
our frozen eyes unribboned   through the storm
we could have stitched that blueness   together   like a quilt

You come (I know this) with your love   your loss
strapped to your body   with your tape-recorder   camera
ice-pick   against advisement
to give us burial in the snow   and in your mind
While my body lies out here
flashing like a prism   into your eyes
how could you sleep   You climbed here for yourself
we climbed for ourselves

When you have buried us   told your story
ours does not end   we stream
into the unfinished   the unbegun
the possible
Every cell's core of heat   pulsed out of us
into the thin air   of the universe
the armature of rock beneath these snows
this mountain   which has taken   the imprint of our minds
through changes elemental and minute
as those we underwent
to bring each other here
choosing ourselves   each other   and this life
whose every breath   and grasp   and further foothold
is somewhere   still enacted   and continuing

Adrienne Rich   195

In the diary I wrote: *Now we are ready*
and each of us knows it   I have never loved
like this   I have never seen
my own forces so taken up and shared
and given back
After the long training   the early sieges
we are moving almost effortlessly in our love

In the diary as the wind   began to tear
at the tents over us   I wrote:
We know now we have always been in danger
down in our separateness
and now up here together   but till now
we had not touched our strength

In the diary torn from my fingers I had written:
What does love mean
what does it mean   "to survive"
A cable of blue fire ropes our bodies
burning together in the snow   We will not live
to settle for less   We have dreamed of this
all of our lives

RAINER MARIA RILKE

AUSTRIA • 1875–1926

My husband introduced me to this poem twenty years ago. I knew Rilke's work, but had not experienced it. That is the importance of this work to me: that I have let it into my life, lived with it, heard it in my head, listened to it inwardly these twenty years.

—Marsha McDonald, 42, Artist/Decorative Painter, Milwaukee, Wisconsin

Initiation

Whoever you are, go out into the evening,
leaving your room, of which you know each bit;
your house is the last before the infinite,
whoever you are.
Then with your eyes that wearily
scarce lift themselves from the worn-out door-stone
slowly you raise a shadowy black tree
and fix it on the sky: slender, alone.
And you have made the world (and it shall grow
and ripen as a word, unspoken, still).
When you have grasped its meaning with your will,
then tenderly your eyes will let it go . . .

Translated from the German by C. F. McIntyre

I first read this poem when I was a freshman at the college where Randall Jarrell (the poem's translator) had taught until his untimely death the year before. It seemed to have that nostalgia mixed with sadness that so epitomizes adolescence. Yet I have grown up through the sadness of the poem to appreciate it for the fine translation. I actually memorized it and said it aloud for a time, it had such a personal resonance to me during those late '60s years of tumult.

—Sue Burroughs Field, 54, Office Manager, Chapel Hill, North
  Carolina

Requiem for the Death of a Boy

Why did I print upon myself the names
Of Elephant and Dog and Cow
So far off now, already so long ago,
And Zebra, too. . . . what for, what for?
What holds me now
Climbs like a water line
Up past all that. What help was it to know
I was, if I could never press
Through what's soft, what's hard, and come at last
Behind them, to the face that understands?

And these beginning hands—

Sometimes you'd say: "He promises. . . ."
Yes, I promised. But what I promised you,
That was never what I felt afraid of.
Sometimes I'd sit against the house for hours
And look up at a bird.
If only I could have turned into the looking!
It lifted me, it flew me, how my eyes
Were open up there then! But I didn't love anybody.
Loving was misery—
Don't you see, I wasn't we,
And I was so much bigger
Than a man, I was my own danger,
And, inside it, I was the seed.

A little seed. The street can have it.
The wind can have it. I give it away.
Because that we all sat there so together—
I never did believe that. No, honestly.
You talked, you laughed, but none of you were ever
Inside the talking or the laughing. No.
The sugar bowl, a glass of milk
Would never waver the way you would waver.
The apple lay there. Sometimes it felt so good
To hold tight to it, a hard ripe apple.
The big table, the coffee-cups that never moved—
They were good, how peaceful they made the year!
And my toy did me good too, sometimes.
It was as reliable, almost, as the others,
Only not so peaceful. It stood halfway
Between me and my hat, in watchfulness forever.
There was a wooden horse, there was a rooster,
There was the doll with only one leg.
I did so much for them.
I made the sky small when they saw it
Because almost from the start I understood
How alone a wooden horse is. You can make one,
A wooden horse, one any size.
It gets painted, and later on you pull it,
And it's the real street it pounds down, then.
When you call it a horse, why isn't it a lie?
Because you feel that you're a horse, a little,
And grow all maney, shiny, grow four legs—
So as to grow, some day, into a man?
But wasn't I wood a little, too,
For its sake, and grew hard and quiet
And looked out at it from an emptier face?

I almost think we traded places.
Whenever I would see the brook I'd race it,
And the brook raced, too, and I would run away.
Whenever I saw something that could ring, I rang,
And whenever something sang I played for it.
I made myself at home with everything.
Only everything was satisfied without me

And got sadder, hung about with me.

Now, all at once, we're separated.
Do the lessons and the questions start again?
Or, now, ought I to say
What it was like with you?—That worries me.
The house? I never got it right, exactly.
The rooms? Oh, there were so many things, so many.
. . . Mother, *who* was the dog really?
That in the forest we would come on berries—
Even that seems, now, extraordinary.

Surely there're some other children
Who've died, to come play with me. They're always dying;
Lie there in bed, like me, and never do get well.

Well. . . . How funny that sounds, here.
Does it mean something, still?
Here where I am
No one is ill, I think.
Since my sore throat, so long ago already—

Here everyone is like a just-poured drink.

But the ones who drink us I still haven't seen.

Translated from the German by Randall Jarrell

Rainer Maria Rilke

Edwin Arlington Robinson

UNITED STATES • 1869–1935

I was raised on a Northwoods farm in northern Wisconsin, and the imagery in this poem, the perfect harvest, has deep meaning for me. Beyond that, the poem speaks of the magic the change of seasons works on all of us.
—June Kraeft, 70, Writer, Bethlehem, Connecticut

The Sheaves

Where long the shadows of the wind had rolled,
Green wheat was yielding to the change assigned;
And as by some vast magic undivined
The world was turning slowly into gold.
Like nothing that was ever bought or sold
It waited there, the body and the mind;
And with a mighty meaning of a kind
That tells the more the more it is not told.

So in a land where all days are not fair,
Fair days went on till on another day
A thousand golden sheaves were lying there,
Shining and still, but not for long to stay—
As if a thousand girls with golden hair
Might rise from where they slept and go away.

The Unforgiven

When he, who is the unforgiven,
Beheld her first, he found her fair:
No promise ever dreamt in heaven
Could then have lured him anywhere
That would have been away from there;
And all his wits had lightly striven,
Foiled with her voice, and eyes, and hair.

There's nothing in the saints and sages
To meet the shafts her glances had,
Or such as hers have had for ages
To blind a man till he be glad,
And humble him till he be mad.
The story would have many pages,
And would be neither good nor bad.

And, having followed, you would find him
Where properly the play begins;
But look for no red light behind him—
No fumes of many-colored sins,
Fanned high by screaming violins.
God knows what good it was to blind him,
Or whether man or woman wins.

And by the same eternal token,
Who knows just how it will all end?—
This drama of hard words unspoken,
This fireside farce, without a friend
Or enemy to comprehend
What augurs when two lives are broken,
And fear finds nothing left to mend.

Edwin Arlington Robinson

He stares in vain for what awaits him,
And sees in Love a coin to toss;
He smiles, and her cold hush berates him
Beneath his hard half of the cross;
They wonder why it ever was;
And she, the unforgiving, hates him
More for her lack than for her loss.

He feeds with pride his indecision,
And shrinks from what will not occur,
Bequeathing with infirm decision
His ashes to the days that were,
Before she made him prisoner;
And labors to retrieve the vision
That he must once have had of her.

He waits, and there awaits an ending,
And he knows neither what nor when;
But no magicians are attending
To make him see as he saw then,
And he will never find again
The face that once had been the rending
Of all his purpose among men.

He blames her not, nor does he chide her,
And she has nothing new to say;
If he were Bluebeard he could hide her,
But that's not written in the play,
And there will be no change to-day;
Although, to the serene outsider,
There still would seem to be a way.

THEODORE ROETHKE

UNITED STATES · 1908–1963

Ahhh . . . Sly, sexy, metaphysical, funky, satirical, beautiful . . . it opened up that space in my chest and gave me deep pleasure. "I measure time by how a body sways." Indeed!
—Rick Pernod, 45, Professor, Bronx, New York

I Knew a Woman

I knew a woman, lovely in her bones,
When small birds sighed, she would sigh back at them;
Ah, when she moved, she moved more ways than one:
The shapes a bright container can contain!
Of her choice virtues only gods should speak,
Or English poets who grew up on Greek
(I'd have them sing in chorus, cheek to cheek).

How well her wishes went! She stroked my chin,
She taught me Turn, and Counter-turn, and Stand;
She taught me Touch, that undulant white skin;
I nibbled meekly from her proffered hand;
She was the sickle; I, poor I, the rake,
Coming behind her for her pretty sake
(But what prodigious mowing we did make).

Love likes a gander, and adores a goose:
Her full lips pursed, the errant note to seize;
She played it quick, she played it light and loose;
My eyes, they dazzled at her flowing knees;
Her several parts could keep a pure repose,
Or one hip quiver with a mobile nose
(She moved in circles, and those circles moved).

Let seed be grass, and grass turn into hay:
I'm martyr to a motion not my own;
What's freedom for? To know eternity.
I swear she cast a shadow white as stone.
But who would count eternity in days?
These old bones live to learn her wanton ways:
(I measure time by how a body sways).

Theodore Roethke

In a Dark Time

In a dark time, the eye begins to see,
I meet my shadow in the deepening shade;
I hear my echo in the echoing wood—
A lord of nature weeping to a tree.
I live between the heron and the wren,
Beasts of the hill and serpents of the den.

What's madness but nobility of soul
At odds with circumstance? The day's on fire!
I know the purity of pure despair,
My shadow pinned against a sweating wall.
That place among the rocks—is it a cave,
Or winding path? The edge is what I have.

A steady storm of correspondences!
A night flowing with birds, a ragged moon,
And in broad day the midnight come again!
A man goes far to find out what he is—
Death of the self in a long, tearless night,
All natural shapes blazing unnatural light.

Dark, dark my light, and darker my desire.
My soul, like some heat-maddened summer fly,
Keeps buzzing at the sill. Which I is *I?*
A fallen man, I climb out of my fear.
The mind enters itself, and God the mind,
And one is One, free in the tearing wind.

Theodore Roethke

The Sloth

In moving-slow he has no Peer.
You ask him something in his Ear,
He thinks about it for a Year;

And, then, before he says a Word
There, upside down (unlike a Bird),
He will assume that you have Heard—

A most Ex-as-per-at-ing Lug.
But should you call his manner Smug,
He'll sigh and give his Branch a Hug;

Then off again to Sleep he goes,
Still swaying gently by his Toes,
And you just *know* he knows he knows.

MURIEL RUKEYSER

UNITED STATES • 1912–1980

When I was fourteen and out of sorts, I stumbled across this poem. It was in an anthology I bought from a discount bin. Her questions were so poignant to me, because I felt the need to reach out to someone. I felt alone and the poem made me feel significant, loved—the narrator's voice so tender, so sweet, that I never forgot it.

—Wendolyn Thurston, Asheville, North Carolina

Effort at Speech Between Two People

  :   Speak to me.   Take my hand.   What are you now?
     I will tell you all.   I will conceal nothing.
     When I was three, a little child read a story about a rabbit
     who died, in the story, and I crawled under a chair :
     a pink rabbit : it was my birthday, and a candle
     burnt a sore spot on my finger, and I was told to be happy.

  :   Oh, grow to know me.   I am not happy.   I will be open:
     Now I am thinking of white sails against a sky like music,
     like glad horns blowing, and birds tilting, and an arm about me.
     There was one I loved, who wanted to live, sailing.

  :   Speak to me.   Take my hand.   What are you now?
     When I was nine, I was fruitily sentimental,
     fluid : and my widowed aunt played Chopin,
     and I bent my head on the painted woodwork, and wept.
     I want now to be close to you.   I would
     link the minutes of my days close, somehow, to your days.

  :   I am not happy.   I will be open.
     I have liked lamps in evening corners, and quiet poems.
     There has been fear in my life.   Sometimes I speculate
     On what a tragedy his life was, really.

  :   Take my hand.   Fist my mind in your hand.   What are
        you now?
     When I was fourteen, I had dreams of suicide,
     and I stood at a steep window, at sunset, hoping toward
          death :

if the light had not melted clouds and plains to beauty,
if light had not transformed that day, I would have leapt.
I am unhappy.   I am lonely.   Speak to me.

:   I will be open.   I think he never loved me:
he loved the bright beaches, the little lips of foam
that ride small waves, he loved the veer of gulls:
he said with a gay mouth: I love you.   Grow to know me.

:   What are you now?   If we could touch one another,
if these our separate entities could come to grips,
clenched like a Chinese puzzle . . . yesterday
I stood in a crowded street that was live with people,
and no one spoke a word, and the morning shone.
Everyone silent, moving. . . . Take my hand.   Speak to me.

                                                      Muriel Rukeyser

SAPPHO

GREECE • 612 B.C.E.–?

I think this poem shows that love is so powerful an emotion that it can take complete control over your body and mind and heart. Love is like an animal—a snake that cannot be tamed or controlled.

—Jennifer Toth, 20, Student/Movie Theater Manager, Harrisonburg,
   Virginia

With his venom

With his venom

Irresistible
and bittersweet

that loosener
of limbs, Love

reptile-like
strikes me down

Translated from the Greek by Mary Barnard

DELMORE SCHWARTZ

UNITED STATES · 1913–1966

*The title attracts someone who is tired and unhappy, which is how I felt
when I started reading it.*
—Molly Hutton, 21, Student, Norfolk, Virginia

Tired and Unhappy, You Think of Houses

Tired and unhappy, you think of houses
Soft-carpeted and warm in the December evening,
While snow's white pieces fall past the window,
And the orange firelight leaps.
                                    A young girl sings
That song of Gluck where Orpheus pleads with Death;
Her elders watch, nodding their happiness
To see time fresh again in her self-conscious eyes:
The servants bring the coffee, the children retire,
Elder and younger yawn and go to bed,
The coals fade and glow, rose and ashen,
It is time to shake yourself and break this
Banal dream, and turn your head
Where the underground is charged, where the weight
Of the lean buildings is seen,
Where close in the subway rush; anonymous
In the audience, well-dressed or mean,
So many surround you, ringing your fate,
Caught in an anger exact as a machine!

SIR WALTER SCOTT

SCOTLAND • 1771–1832

I discovered this poem at the St. Louis Art Museum one April. I came across a painting of a perfect golden dog beside the still gray-blue figure of a fallen man. It was set in a lonely mountain place. As I drew closer to read the description of the work I was moved to tears in an instant by the poem and the apparently true story this painting illustrates: in 1805, a young man perished while wandering on the mountain Hellvellyn in Scotand with his dog. When his remains were found three months later, they were guarded still by the faithful dog. I bought a book to have a copy of the poem. I think the most transcendent experiences are those where we are dwarfed by forces greater than ourselves—the momentousness of nature, beauty, or the faithfulness of a dog.

—Nancy Kilpatrick, 50, Federal Manager, Arlington, Virginia

Hellvellyn

> *In the spring of 1805, a young gentleman of talents, and of a most amiable disposition, perished by losing his way on the mountain Hellvellyn. His remains were not discovered till three months afterwards, when they were found guarded by a faithful terrier-bitch, his constant attendant during frequent solitary rambles through the wilds of Cumberland and Westmoreland.*

I climbed the dark brow of the mighty Hellvellyn,
    Lakes and mountains beneath me gleamed misty and wide;
All was still, save by fits, when the eagle was yelling,
    And starting around me the echoes replied.
On the right, Striden-edge round the Red-tarn was bending,
And Catchedicam its left verge was defending,
One huge nameless rock in the front was ascending,
    When I marked the sad spot where the wanderer had died.

Dark green was that spot mid the brown mountain heather,
    Where the Pilgrim of Nature lay stretched in decay,
Like the corpse of an outcast abandoned to weather,
    Till the mountain-winds wasted the tenantless clay.
Nor yet quite deserted, though lonely extended,

For, faithful in death, his mute favourite attended,
The much-loved remains of her master defended,
   And chased the hill-fox and the raven away.

How long didst thou think that his silence was slumber?
   When the wind waved his garment, how oft didst thou start?
How many long days and long weeks didst thou number,
   Ere he faded before thee, the friend of thy heart?
And, oh, was it meet, that,—no requiem read o'er him,—
No mother to weep, and no friend to deplore him,
And thou, little guardian, alone stretched before him,—
   Unhonoured the Pilgrim from life should depart?

When a Prince to the fate of the Peasant has yielded,
   The tapestry waves dark round the dim-lighted hall;
With scutcheons of silver the coffin is shielded,
   And pages stand mute by the canopied pall:
Through the courts, at deep midnight, the torches are gleaming;
In the proudly-arched chapel the banners are beaming;
Far adown the long aisle sacred music is streaming,
   Lamenting a Chief of the People should fall.

But meeter for thee, gentle lover of nature,
   To lay down thy head like the meek mountain lamb,
When, wildered, he drops from some cliff huge in stature,
   And draws his last sob by the side of his dam.
And more stately thy couch by this desert lake lying,
Thy obsequies sung by the grey plover flying,
With one faithful friend but to witness thy dying,
   In the arms of Hellvellyn and Catchedicam.

                                    Sir Walter Scott

ANNE SEXTON

UNITED STATES • 1928–1974

I have read Anne Sexton faithfully since I was fourteen years old. In 1990, my grandmother passed away. She was the woman who raised me. I could not imagine living life without my "anchor." I searched for a way to deal with the pain of her loss. One day, while looking for a book of poetry to dissolve into, I went back to an Anne Sexton poem that always intrigued me. I read and reread it, and felt my feelings brought to life and acknowledged through her words. At the age of fifteen, nothing seemed more true and more real than this poem.

—Holli-Marie Hansen, 26, Teacher, Bushkill, Pennsylvania

The Truth the Dead Know

*For my mother, born March 1902, died March 1959,
and my father, born February 1900, died June 1959*

Gone, I say and walk from church,
refusing the stiff procession to the grave,
letting the dead ride alone in the hearse.
It is June. I am tired of being brave.

We drive to the Cape. I cultivate
myself where the sun gutters from the sky,
where the sea swings in like an iron gate
and we touch. In another country people die.

My darling, the wind falls in like stones
from the whitehearted water and when we touch
we enter touch entirely. No one's alone.
Men kill for this, or for as much.

And what of the dead? They lie without shoes
in their stone boats. They are more like stone
than the sea would be if it stopped. They refuse
to be blessed, throat, eye and knucklebone.

WILLIAM SHAKESPEARE

ENGLAND · 1564–1616

That the poem begins by referring to an actor who forgets his lines makes it
visceral and immediate. As an actor, it is comforting for me to think that
even our master playwright knew firsthand what stage fright felt like.
—Sherri Allen, 37, Actor, Del Mar, California

As an unperfect actor on the stage

(*Sonnets* 23)

As an unperfect actor on the stage,
Who with his fear is put besides his part,
Or some fierce thing replete with too much rage,
Whose strength's abundance weakens his own heart,
So I, for fear of trust, forget to say
The perfect ceremony of love's rite,
And in mine own love's strength seem to decay,
O'ercharged with burden of mine own love's might.
Oh, let my books be then the eloquence
And dumb presagers of my speaking breast,
Who plead for love, and look for recompense,
More than that tongue that more hath more expressed.
Oh, learn to read what silent love hath writ.
To hear with eyes belongs to love's fine wit.

In high school I was assigned Sonnet 73 to memorize. It was a struggle. I forgot words, left out lines, stumbled over the syntax. But I always appreciated the first two stanzas. The first is about a time of year—late autumn. I have always loved the quiet sadness of rainy November after the brilliance of October. The second is about a favorite time of day—deepening twilight, when the sky is purple, and you can see the edge of night approaching. The third stanza I did not understand well until this year. I read the poem again after cancer struck my family. It is about a time of life, just before death, when the fire is burning out, bright embers on ash, coming to an end. It is about passion still burning. My husband is passionate about his teaching, his art, his family. He is finishing his life in the same way he has lived it—full of passion, love, and humor. Now the couplet no longer seems obvious and preachy as it once did. Now it reads as the anthem of our family as we pull in close, cherishing the finite brief time we have together.

—Christine McDonnell, 53, Teacher, Brookline, Massachusetts

That time of year thou mayst in me behold

(*Sonnets* 73)

That time of year thou mayst in me behold
When yellow leaves, or none, or few, do hang
Upon those boughs which shake against the cold,
Bare ruined choirs where late the sweet birds sang.
In me thou see'st the twilight of such day
As after sunset fadeth in the west,
Which by and by black night doth take away,
Death's second self, that seals up all in rest.
In me thou see'st the glowing of such fire
That on the ashes of his youth doth lie,
As the deathbed whereon it must expire,
Consumed with that which it was nourished by.
This thou perceiv'st, which makes thy love more strong,
To love that well which thou must leave ere long.

William Shakespeare

My father had a small shoe store, and went bankrupt when I was nine years old. My mother had died when I was eight months old in the influenza epidemic of 1918. I was in an orphanage for a while, but I ran away so many times that they wouldn't take me back, and I lived with my father in a hotel. . . . It was during that time that I had an English teacher, Mrs. Frasier, who required all the classmates to choose a poem and get it by heart. . . . This is the poem which I learned when I was in seventh grade and what it meant to me at that time was that feeling of being in such misfortune—my experience in the orphanage—and the fact that a situation can turn around so quickly, that business of being well down in the depths and being able to come up.

—Daniel McCall, 81, Retired Anthropologist, Boston, Massachusetts

When, in disgrace with Fortune and men's eyes

DVD, Track 11

(*Sonnets* 29)

When, in disgrace with Fortune and men's eyes,
I all alone beweep my outcast state,
And trouble deaf heaven with my bootless cries,
And look upon myself and curse my fate,
Wishing me like to one more rich in hope,
Featured like him, like him with friends possessed,
Desiring this man's art, and that man's scope,
With what I most enjoy contented least;
Yet in these thoughts myself almost despising,
Haply I think on thee, and then my state,
Like to the lark at break of day arising
From sullen earth, sings hymns at heaven's gate;
For thy sweet love rememb'red such wealth brings,
That then I scorn to change my state with kings.

William Shakespeare

The poem is in praise of children. I work in a children's hospital and care for sick children. I also have three children of my own who mean more to me than anything in my life.

—Robert DiMauro, 64, Pediatric Radiologist, Honolulu, Hawaii

When forty winters shall besiege thy brow

(*Sonnets* 2)

When forty winters shall besiege thy brow
And dig deep trenches in thy beauty's field,
Thy youth's proud livery, so gazed on now,
Will be a tattered weed, of small worth held.
Then being asked where all thy beauty lies,
Where all the treasure of thy lusty days,
To say within thine own deep-sunken eyes
Were an all-eating shame and thriftless praise.
How much more praise deserved thy beauty's use
If thou couldst answer, "This fair child of mine
Shall sum my count and make my old excuse,"
Proving his beauty by succession thine!
This were to be new-made when thou art old,
And see thy blood warm when thou feel'st it cold.

William Shakespeare

PERCY BYSSHE SHELLEY

ENGLAND · 1792–1822

My husband Jim and I were married when I was fifty-seven and he was sixty-five. In our ceremony, Jim read the beginning to me and I to him the ending of this poem. We both felt we had lived our lives all the years before to be joined together, and the poem said everything we felt in our hearts.
—Phyllis Burnett-Blackwell, 58, Artist, Old Hickory, Tennessee

Love's Philosophy

The fountains mingle with the river,
   And the rivers with the ocean;
The winds of heaven mix forever
   With a sweet emotion;
Nothing in the world is single;
   All things by a law divine
In one another's being mingle:
   Why not I with thine?

See the mountains kiss high heaven,
   And the waves clasp one another;
No sister flower would be forgiven
   If it disdained its brother;
And the sunlight clasps the earth,
   And the moonbeams kiss the sea;
What are all these kissings worth,
   If thou kiss not me?

*My grandparents came to America from Ischia, an island in Italy. Shelley
spent time on this island. His work connects me with my grandparents who
passed away before I could get to know them. The beautiful imagery and
Shelley's melancholy conjure my grandmother's description of her childhood
home as a place of impressive beauty, but long abandoned.*

—John Dilustro, 32, Postdoctoral Fellow in Ecology, Columbus,
    Georgia

Stanzas written in Dejection—December 1818, Near Naples

The Sun is warm, the sky is clear,
The waves are dancing fast and bright,
Blue isles and snowy mountains wear
The purple noon's transparent might,
The breath of the moist earth is light
Around its unexpanded buds;
Like many a voice of one delight
The winds, the birds, the Ocean-floods;
The City's voice itself is soft, like Solitude's.

I see the Deep's untrampled floor
With green and purple seaweeds strown;
I see the waves upon the shore
Like light dissolved in star-showers, thrown;
I sit upon the sands alone;
The lightning of the noontide Ocean
Is flashing round me, and a tone
Arises from its measured motion,
How sweet! did any heart now share in my emotion.

Alas, I have nor hope nor health
Nor peace within nor calm around,
Nor that content surpassing wealth
The sage in meditation found,
And walked with inward glory crowned;
Nor fame nor power nor love nor leisure—
Others I see whom these surround,

Smiling they live and call life pleasure:
To me that cup has been dealt in another measure.

Yet now despair itself is mild,
Even as the winds and waters are;
I could lie down like a tired child
And weep away the life of care
Which I have borne and yet must bear
Till Death like Sleep might steal on me,
And I might feel in the warm air
My cheek grow cold, and hear the Sea
Breathe o'er my dying brain its last monotony.

Some might lament that I were cold,
As I, when this sweet day is gone,
Which my lost heart, too soon grown old,
Insults with this untimely moan—
They might lament,—for I am one
Whom men love not, and yet regret;
Unlike this day, which, when the Sun
Shall on its stainless glory set,
Will linger though enjoyed, like joy in Memory yet.

Percy Bysshe Shelley

EDMUND SPENSER

ENGLAND · 1552–1599

I like this poem for a number of reasons, primarily because it reminds me why "sweet with sour" is actually better than sweet or sour alone.
—Lauren Hatch, Memphis, Tennessee

Sweet is the rose, but grows upon a brere

(*Amoretti* 26)

Sweet is the rose, but grows upon a brere;
Sweet is the juniper, but sharp his bough;
Sweet is the eglantine, but pricketh near;
Sweet is the firbloom, but his branches rough;
Sweet is the cypress, but his rind is tough;
Sweet is the nut, but bitter is his pill;
Sweet is the broom-flower, but yet sour enough;
And sweet is moly, but his root is ill.
So every sweet with sour is tempered still,
That maketh it be coveted the more;
For easy things, that may be got at will,
Most sorts of men do set but little store.
Why then should I account of little pain,
That endless pleasure shall unto me gain?

WILLIAM STAFFORD

UNITED STATES · 1914–1993

Occasionally, the net of my memory snares a moment of my mother's life—
a verse she recited in childhood and then taught to me, a tune she hummed
while quilting, an expression she used to excuse uneven hems or crooked
seams. I hold the memory in my mind and pass it on to my granddaughter.
When this happens, I always think of this poem by William Stafford, a
poem that weaves together the past, present, and future while describing
happiness more succinctly and vividly than anything else I have ever read.
—Debra Griffin, 47, Secretary, Borger, Texas

The Gift

Time wants to show you a different country. It's the one
that your life conceals, the one waiting outside
when curtains are drawn, the one Grandmother hinted at
in her crochet design, the one almost found
over at the edge of the music, after the sermon.

It's the way life is, and you have it, a few years given.
You get killed now and then, violated
in various ways. (And sometimes it's turn about.)
You get tired of that. Long-suffering, you wait
and pray, and maybe good things come—maybe
the hurt slackens and you hardly feel it any more.
You have a breath without pain. It is called happiness.

It's a balance, the taking and passing along,
the composting of where you've been and how people
and weather treated you. It's a country where
you already are, bringing where you have been.
Time offers this gift in its millions of ways,
turning the world, moving the air, calling,
every morning, "Here, take it, it's yours."

GERALD STERN

UNITED STATES • B. 1925

This poem on one level is about the sadness of time inexorably passing, but on another it's a celebration of the things in our lives—for Stern, old shirts relegated to the back of the closet. Reading the poem I was reminded once again of how so often it's the "little things" that have the quietest but loudest voices.

—John Bailey, 42, Baltimore, Maryland

The Shirt Poem

It is ten years since I have seen these shirts
screaming from their hangers, crying for blood and money.
They shake their empty arms
and grow stiff as they wait for the light to come.
I open the door an inch at a time to let them out
and start candles all over the room to soothe them.
—Gone is sweetness in that closet, gone is the dream
of brotherhood, the affectionate meeting
of thinkers and workers inside a rented hall.
Gone are the folding chairs, gone forever
the sacred locking of elbows under the two flags.

On Sunday night they used to sing for hours
before the speeches. Once the rabbis joined them
and religion and economics were finally combined in exile.
"Death is a defect," they sang, and threw their hats
on the floor. "We will save nature from death,"
they shouted, and ended up dancing on the small stage,
the dark crows and the speckled doves finally arm in arm.

They will never come back—in a thousand years;
it is not like bringing a forest back, putting a truckload
of nitrogen in the soil, burning some brush,
planting seedlings, measuring distance—
these are people, whose secret habits we no longer know,
how they tore their bread and what designs they made on the
    tablecloth,

what they thought about as they stared through the warped glass,
what the melting ice meant to them.

Poor dead ones! Forgive me for the peace I feel as I walk out
to the mailbox. Forgive me for the rich life I lead.
Forgive me for the enormous budget and the bureaucracy and the
    permanent army.
When I come home from New York City I stand outside
for twenty minutes and look out at the lights.
Upstairs the shirts are howling and snapping,
marching back and forth in front of the silver radiator.
In a minute I will be up there closing doors
and turning on lamps.

I will take the papers out of my coat pocket
and put them in their slots.
I will think of you with your own papers and your rubber bands.
What is my life if not a substitute for yours,
and my dream a substitute for your dream?
Lord, how it has changed, how we have
made ourselves strange, how embarrassing the words
sound to us, how clumsy and half-hearted we are.

I want to write it down before it's forgotten,
how we lived, what we believed in;
most of all to remember the giants
and how they walked, always with white hair,
always with long white hair hanging down over their collars,
always with red faces, always bowing and listening,
their heads floating as they moved through the small crowd.

Outside the wind is blowing
and the snow is piling up against the pillars.
I could go back in a minute to the synagogue in Beechview
or the Carnegie Library on the North Side.
I could turn and shake hands with the tiny man
sitting beside me and wish him peace.
I could stand in front and watch the stained-glass
window rattle in its frame and the guest speaker
climb into the back seat of his car.

I am writing about the past because there was
still affection left then, and other sorrows;
because I believed my white silk scarf could save me,
and my all-day walks;
because when I opened my window the smell
of snow made me tremble with pleasure;
because I was a head taller than the tiny man sitting next to me;
because I was always the youngest;
because I believed in Shelley;
because I carried my entire memory along with me in the
      summer;
because I stared at the old men with loving eyes;
because I studied their fallen shoulders and their huge hands;
because I found relief only in my drawings;
because I knew the color and texture of every rug and every chair
and every lampshade in my first house.

Give this to Rabbi Kook who always arrived
with his clothes on fire and stood between the mourners,
singing songs against death in all three languages
at the crowded wall, in the dark sunlight.

And give this to Malatesta who believed in
the perfect world and lived in it as he moved
from country to country, for sixty years, tasting the
bread, tasting the meat, always working,
cursing the Church, cursing the State,
seeing through everything, always seeing the heart
and what it wanted, the beautiful cramped heart.

My shirts are fine. They dance
by themselves along the river
and bleed a little as they fall down on the dirty glass.
If they had knees they would try to
crawl back up the hill and stop the trucks
or march back and forth singing their swamp songs.
They see me coming and fly up to the roof;
they are like prehistoric birds,
half leaping, half sailing by.
They scream with cold, they break through the hall window

and knock over baskets and push open doors
until they stand there in place, in back of the neckties,
beside the cold plaster, in the dust
above the abandoned shoes, weeping in silence,
moaning in exhaustion,
getting ready again to live in darkness.

Gerald Stern

WALLACE STEVENS

UNITED STATES • 1879–1955

This poem reminded me of my father. He was quite a responsible person, but perhaps overly so and it taxed his spirit.

—Katherine Donahue, 54, Rare Books Librarian, Los Angeles, California

Disillusionment of Ten O'Clock

The houses are haunted
By white night-gowns.
None are green,
Or purple with green rings,
Or green with yellow rings,
Or yellow with blue rings.
None of them are strange,
With socks of lace
And beaded ceintures.
People are not going
To dream of baboons and periwinkles.
Only, here and there, an old sailor,
Drunk and asleep in his boots,
Catches tigers
In red weather.

This poem has always conjured images of my childhood spent playing in the deepening twilight shadows of summer. We used to scurry around in the dense shrubbery "forts" of our suburban yards hiding from our enemies, listening intently so we wouldn't be ambushed. It was wonderfully cool and still. Although the rabbit in this poem pays the ultimate price for his self-absorption, his view of the world is gloriously childlike. He is one with his time and space. The images are so vivid and the rhythm so hypnotic, if I close my eyes I swear can I can still hear crickets.

—Cynthia Bazinet, 41, Teacher, Holden, Massachusetts

A Rabbit as King of the Ghosts

The difficulty to think at the end of day,
When the shapeless shadow covers the sun
And nothing is left except light on your fur—

There was the cat slopping its milk all day,
Fat cat, red tongue, green mind, white milk
And August the most peaceful month.

To be, in the grass, in the peacefullest time,
Without that monument of cat,
The cat forgotten in the moon;

And to feel that the light is a rabbit-light,
In which everything is meant for you
And nothing need be explained;

Then there is nothing to think of. It comes of itself;
And east rushes west and west rushes down,
No matter. The grass is full

And full of yourself. The trees around are for you,
The whole of the wideness of night is for you,
A self that touches all edges,

You become a self that fills the four corners of night.
The red cat hides away in the fur-light
And there you are humped high, humped up,

You are humped higher and higher, black as stone—
You sit with your head like a carving in space
And the little green cat is a bug in the grass.

ROBERT LOUIS STEVENSON

SCOTLAND • 1850–1894

*This poem has a special meaning to me. As a child, my family underwent
many trials and many responsibilities were given to me. Some have told me
I never had a childhood. I disagree. I remember my mom reading library
books under the kitchen table that had a sheet draped over it. I remember
climbing trees after school and writing adventure stories about kids in far-
off places in my spare time. Sometimes now my mom tells me I'm so goofy
that no one would ever know I'm almost eighteen years old. That's good
because I believe that there is a part of me that will never grow up. Some
say Stevenson didn't have a childhood since he was so sickly. I disagree. He
knew how to have fun and still enjoy life's blessings. His poems bring out
the childhood in all of us.*

—Melissa Nelson, 17, Student, New Albany, Indiana

My Shadow

I have a little shadow that goes in and out with me,
And what can be the use of him is more than I can see.
He is very, very like me from the heels up to the head;
And I see him jump before me, when I jump into my bed.

The funniest thing about him is the way he likes to grow—
Not at all like proper children, which is always very slow;
For he sometimes shoots up taller like an india-rubber ball,
And he sometimes gets so little that there's none of him at all.

He hasn't got a notion of how children ought to play,
And can only make a fool of me in every sort of way.
He stays so close beside me, he's a coward you can see;
I'd think shame to stick to nursie as that shadow sticks to me!

One morning, very early, before the sun was up,
I rose and found the shining dew on every buttercup;
But my lazy little shadow, like an arrant sleepy-head,
Had stayed at home behind me and was fast asleep in bed.

MARK STRAND

UNITED STATES • B. 1934

*It speaks to me with honesty and directness as it did when I first read it in
1977. It was a year of change, a year in which I seemed to be both more
and less than myself simultaneously. It touched those fields of absence in me
as I worked my way through a divorce and returned to school while caring
for my three children. It is one of those poems which, when read silently
from the page, touched something so personal I could hardly believe it. Yet,
when read aloud, with its no-nonsense directness, its musical repetition and
joy of rhyme, it became an anthem.*
—Sunny Solomon, 56, Paralegal, Concord, California

Keeping Things Whole

In a field
I am the absence
of field.
This is
always the case.
Wherever I am
I am what is missing.

When I walk
I part the air
and always
the air moves in
to fill the spaces
where my body's been.

We all have reasons
for moving.
I move
to keep things whole.

MAY SWENSON

UNITED STATES · 1919–1989

When I was a child living on the Kansas prairie, our nearest neighbors were a mile away. My brother, sister, and I did not have a lot of toys or other children to play with. Of course we didn't have TV; but we did have vivid imaginations! This poem brings back pleasant memories of "riding the range" on my favorite stick horse, Buck.
—Phyllis Stanley, 63, Retired Teacher, Augusta, Kansas

The Centaur

The summer that I was ten—
Can it be there was only one
summer that I was ten? It must

have been a long one then—
each day I'd go out to choose
a fresh horse from my stable

which was a willow grove
down by the old canal.
I'd go on my two bare feet.

But when, with my brother's jackknife,
I had cut me a long limber horse
with a good thick knob for a head,

and peeled him slick and clean
except a few leaves for the tail,
and cinched my brother's belt

around his head for a rein,
I'd straddle and canter him fast
up the grass bank to the path,

trot along in the lovely dust
that talcumed over his hoofs,
hiding my toes, and turning

his feet to swift half-moons.
The willow knob with the strap
jouncing between my thighs

was the pommel and yet the poll
of my nickering pony's head.
My head and my neck were mine,

yet they were shaped like a horse.
My hair flopped to the side
like the mane of a horse in the wind.

My forelock swung in my eyes,
my neck arched and I snorted.
I shied and skittered and reared,

stopped and raised my knees,
pawed at the ground and quivered.
My teeth bared as we wheeled

and swished through the dust again.
I was the horse and the rider,
and the leather I slapped to his rump

spanked my own behind.
Doubled, my two hoofs beat
a gallop along the bank,

the wind twanged in my mane,
my mouth squared to the bit.
And yet I sat on my steed

quiet, negligent riding,
my toes standing the stirrups,
my thighs hugging his ribs.

At a walk we drew up to the porch.
I tethered him to a paling.
Dismounting, I smoothed my skirt

and entered the dusky hall.
My feet on the clean linoleum
left ghostly toes in the hall.

Where have you been? said my mother.
Been riding, I said from the sink,
and filled me a glass of water.

What's that in your pocket? she said.
Just my knife. It weighted my pocket
and stretched my dress awry.

Go tie back your hair, said my mother,
and *Why is your mouth all green?*
*Rob Roy, he pulled some clover
as we crossed the field,* I told her.

Wisława Szymborska

POLAND · B. 1923

My partner Steve was very sick. He'd gotten an AIDS diagnosis and tried all different types of drug treatments, but he was really at the end of the line, and it was a scary time, and it was a difficult time. Szymborska's poem reminded me to treasure the things in our daily life that are the most ordinary, the things that we have here rather than what's out there, the things just like watching TV together, playing Scrabble, reading in bed— the things that we did every day and every night.

—Bill Hayes, 38, Writer, San Francisco, California

Notes from a Nonexistent Himalayan Expedition

DVD, Track 22

So these are the Himalayas.
Mountains racing to the moon.
The moment of their start recorded
on the startling, ripped canvas of the sky.
Holes punched in a desert of clouds.
Thrust into nothing.
Echo—a white mute.
Quiet.

Yeti, down there we've got Wednesday,
bread and alphabets.
Two times two is four.
Roses are red there,
and violets are blue.

Yeti, crime is not all
we're up to down there.
Yeti, not every sentence there
means death.

We've inherited hope—
the gift of forgetting.
You'll see how we give
birth among the ruins.

Yeti, we've got Shakespeare there.
Yeti, we play solitaire
and violin. At nightfall,
we turn lights on, Yeti.

Up here it's neither moon nor earth.
Tears freeze.
Oh Yeti, semi-moonman,
turn back, think again!

I called this to the Yeti
inside four walls of avalanche,
stomping my feet for warmth
on the everlasting
snow.

Translated from the Polish by Stanisław Barańczak and Clare Cavanagh

RABINDRANATH TAGORE

INDIA • 1861–1941

I first read this poem in school as a child, but it was only later that I really understood its meaning. When I was going through a very difficult time of my life as an adult, this poem gave me strength and consolation.
—Jayashree Chatterjee, 52, Librarian, Summit, New Jersey

from *Gitanjali*   DVD, *Track 23*

35

Where the mind is without fear and the head is held high;
    Where knowledge is free;
    Where the world has not been broken up into fragments by
        narrow domestic walls;
    Where words come out from the depth of truth;
    Where tireless striving stretches its arms towards perfection:
    Where the clear stream of reason has not lost its way into the
        dreary desert sand of dead habit;
    Where the mind is led forward by thee into ever-widening
        thought and action—
    Into that heaven of freedom, my Father, let my country
        awake.

39

When the heart is hard and parched up, come upon me with a
    shower of mercy.
    When grace is lost from life, come with a burst of song.
    When tumultuous work raises its din on all sides shutting
        me out from beyond, come to me, my lord of silence,
        with thy peace and rest.
    When my beggarly heart sits crouched, shut up in a corner,
        break open the door, my king, and come with the
        ceremony of a king.
    When desire blinds the mind with delusion and dust, O
        thou holy one, thou wakeful, come with thy light and thy
        thunder.

Translated from the Bengali by Rabindranath Tagore

JAMES TATE

UNITED STATES • B. 1943

A suburb-dweller all my life, I've loved going back to this short poem of Tate's again and again. "Somehow, one expects all that food to rise up out of the canning jars and off the dinner plates and do something, mean something." And, of course, it does and it doesn't, much as life for anyone both does and doesn't mean much.

—John Gallaher, 34, Office Professional, Athens, Ohio

The Sadness of My Neighbors

Somehow, one expects
all that food
to rise up
out of the canning jars
and off the dinner plates
and *do* something,
mean something.

But, alas, it's all
just stuff and more
stuff, without pausing
for an interval
of transformation.

Even family
relationships
go begging
for any illumination.

And yet, there is competence,
there is some quiet
glitter to the surface,
a certain cleanliness,
which means next to

nothing, unless you want
to eat off the floor.

ALFRED, LORD TENNYSON

ENGLAND · 1809–1892

I remember hearing my grandfather read selections of In Memoriam *from the pulpit of the First Universalist Church in Lynn, Massachusetts, during his sermon the Sunday morning after Dr. Martin Luther King was assassinated.*

—Joe Thompson, 55, North Kingstown, Rhode Island

from *In Memoriam A.H.H.*

54

O, yet we trust that somehow good
   Will be the final goal of ill,
   To pangs of nature, sins of will,
Defects of doubt, and taints of blood;

That nothing walks with aimless feet;
   That not one life shall be destroyed,
   Or cast as rubbish to the void,
When God hath made the pile complete;

That not a worm is cloven in vain;
   That not a moth with vain desire
   Is shrivell'd in a fruitless fire,
Or but subserves another's gain.

Behold, we know not anything;
   I can but trust that good shall fall
   At last—far off—at last, to all,
And every winter change to spring.

So runs my dreams; but what am I?
   An infant crying in the night;
   An infant crying for the light,
And with no language but a cry.

Alfred, Lord Tennyson

ERNEST LAWRENCE THAYER

UNITED STATES · 1863–1940

I love baseball—it's my life. I learned to read from looking through my many, many, many baseball cards.

—Lee Samuel, 11, Student, Atlanta, Georgia

Casey at the Bat

DVD, Track 24

The outlook wasn't brilliant for the Mudville nine that day;
The score stood four to two with but one inning more to play.
And then when Cooney died at first, and Barrows did the same,
A sickly silence fell upon the patrons of the game.

A straggling few got up to go in deep despair. The rest
Clung to that hope which springs eternal in the human breast;
They thought if only Casey could but get a whack at that—
We'd put up even money now, with Casey at the bat.

But Flynn preceded Casey, as did also Jimmy Blake,
And the former was a lulu, and the latter was a cake;
So upon that stricken multitude grim melancholy sat,
For there seemed but little chance of Casey's getting to the bat.

But Flynn let drive a single, to the wonderment of all,
And Blake, the much despis-ed, tore the cover off the ball;
And when the dust had lifted, and the men saw what had occurred,
There was Johnnie safe at second and Flynn a-hugging third.

Then from 5,000 throats and more there rose a lusty yell;
It rumbled through the valley, it rattled in the dell;
It knocked upon the mountain and recoiled upon the flat,
For Casey, mighty Casey, was advancing to the bat.

There was ease in Casey's manner as he stepped into his place;
There was pride in Casey's bearing and a smile on Casey's face.
And when, responding to the cheers, he lightly doffed his cap,
No stranger in the crowd could doubt 'twas Casey at the bat.

Ten thousand eyes were on him as he rubbed his hands with dirt;
Five thousand tongues applauded when he wiped them on his shirt.

Then while the writhing pitcher ground the ball into his hip,
Defiance gleamed in Casey's eye, a sneer curled Casey's lip.

And now the leather-covered sphere came hurtling through the air,
And Casey stood a-watching it in haughty grandeur there.
Close by the sturdy batsman the ball unheeded sped—
"That ain't my style," said Casey. "Strike one," the umpire said.

From the benches, black with people, there went up a muffled roar,
Like the beating of the storm-waves on a stern and distant shore.
"Kill him! Kill the umpire!" shouted someone on the stand;
And it's likely they'd have killed him, had not Casey raised his hand.

With a smile of Christian charity great Casey's visage shown;
He stilled the rising tumult; he bade the game go on;
He signaled to the pitcher, and once more the spheroid flew;
But Casey still ignored it, and the umpire said, "Strike two."

"Fraud!" cried the maddened thousands, and echo answered fraud;
But one scornful look from Casey and the audience was awed.
They saw his face grow stern and cold, they saw his muscles strain,
And they knew that Casey wouldn't let that ball go by again.

The sneer is gone from Casey's lip, his teeth are clinched in hate;
He pounds with cruel violence his bat upon the plate.
And now the pitcher holds the ball, and now he lets it go,
And now the air is shattered by the force of Casey's blow.

Oh, somewhere in this favored land the sun is shining bright;
A band is playing somewhere, and somewhere hearts are light.
And somewhere men are laughing, and somewhere children shout;
But there is no joy in Mudville—mighty Casey has struck out.

Ernest Lawrence Thayer

DYLAN THOMAS

WALES • 1914–1953

More than thirty years ago, this poem awoke for me and suddenly became powerful instead of obscure. It is so hard to write about sex—and to write with passion of the hunger of sex, the sorrow of mortality, and the longing of spirit all together, to say what's hard to say, what we all know, but rarely admit.

—Richard Ristow, 56, Providence, Rhode Island

If I were tickled by the rub of love

If I were tickled by the rub of love,
A rooking girl who stole me for her side,
Broke through her straws, breaking my bandaged string,
If the red tickle as the cattle calve
Still set to scratch a laughter from my lung,
I would not fear the apple nor the flood
Nor the bad blood of spring.

Shall it be male or female? say the cells,
And drop the plum like fire from the flesh.
If I were tickled by the hatching hair,
The winging bone that sprouted in the heels,
The itch of man upon the baby's thigh,
I would not fear the gallows nor the axe
Nor the crossed sticks of war.

Shall it be male or female? say the fingers
That chalk the walls with green girls and their men.
I would not fear the muscling-in of love
If I were tickled by the urchin hungers
Rehearsing heat upon a raw-edged nerve.
I would not fear the devil in the loin
Nor the outspoken grave.

If I were tickled by the lovers' rub
That wipes away not crow's-foot nor the lock
Of sick old manhood on the fallen jaws,
Time and the crabs and the sweethearting crib

Would leave me cold as butter for the flies,
The sea of scums could drown me as it broke
Dead on the sweethearts' toes.

This world is half the devil's and my own,
Daft with the drug that's smoking in a girl
And curling round the bud that forks her eye.
An old man's shank one-marrowed with my bone,
And all the herrings smelling in the sea,
I sit and watch the worm beneath my nail
Wearing the quick away.

And that's the rub, the only rub that tickles.
The knobbly ape that swings along his sex
From damp love-darkness and the nurse's twist
Can never raise the midnight of a chuckle,
Nor when he finds a beauty in the breast
Of lover, mother, lovers, or his six
Feet in the rubbing dust.

And what's the rub? Death's feather on the nerve?
Your mouth, my love, the thistle in the kiss?
My Jack of Christ born thorny on the tree?
The words of death are dryer than his stiff.
My wordy wounds are printed with your hair.
I would be tickled by the rub that is:
Man be my metaphor.

My love for this poem came about when I was divorcing a man I still loved. I loved him with all my heart, and I believe he loved me to the best of his ability, but things couldn't continue the way they were. He saw no need for change, so I left. He wanted me back and I felt as though I had kicked him when he was down. I read this poem, and let go.

—April Coen, 23, Deputy Clerk of Court, Kalispell, Montana

You shall not despair

You shall not despair
Because I have forsaken you
Or cast your love aside;
There is a greater love than mine
Which can comfort you
And touch you with softer hands.
I am no longer
Friendly and beautiful to you;
Your body cannot gladden me,
Nor the splendour of your dark hair,
But I do not humiliate you;
You shall be taken sweetly again
And soothed with slow tears;
You shall be loved enough.

Dylan Thomas

R. S. Thomas

WALES · 1913–2000

Like Frost, Thomas demonstrates the way those of us who sometimes feel tired, misplaced, or frightened, can find comfort in Nature's embrace. What better spot could a child rescued from Hitler's Blitzkrieg (or an adult retired from the rat race) wind up in than the peaceful English countryside?
—Ronald Ryner, 56, Retired Teacher, Wall, New Jersey

The Evacuee

She woke up under a loose quilt
Of leaf patterns, woven by the light
At the small window, busy with the boughs
Of a young cherry; but wearily she lay,
Waiting for the syren, slow to trust
Nature's deceptive peace, and then afraid
Of the long silence, she would have crept
Uneasily from the bedroom with its frieze
Of fresh sunlight, had not a cock crowed,
Shattering the surface of that limpid pool
Of stillness, and before the ripples died
One by one in the field's shallows,
The farm awoke with uninhibited din.

And now the noise and not the silence drew her
Down the bare stairs at great speed.
The sounds and voices were a rough sheet
Waiting to catch her, as though she leaped
From a scorched story of the charred past.

And there the table and the gallery
Of farm faces trying to be kind
Beckoned her nearer, and she sat down
Under an awning of salt hams.

And so she grew, a shy bird in the nest
Of welcome that was built about her,
Home now after so long away
In the flowerless streets of the drab town.

The men watched her busy with the hens,
The soft flesh ripening warm as corn
On the sticks of limbs, the grey eyes clear,
Rinsed with dew of their long dread.
The men watched her, and, nodding, smiled
With earth's charity, patient and strong.

MARINA TSVETAEVA

RUSSIA • 1892–1941

*I was raised in a very open spiritual environment where the word "God"
was rarely used, and if it was, it was assumed to have very different mean-
ings for different people. For me, in the context of this poem, it is a collec-
tive term for the higher aspirations of human beings, the nobler values to
which we hold ourselves and our behavior.*
—Alison Alstrom, 31, Bartender/Student, San Francisco, California

Bent with worry

Bent with worry, God
   paused, to smile.
And look, there were many
holy angels with bodies of

the radiance he had
   given them,
some with enormous wings and
others without any,

which is why I weep
   so much
because even more than God
himself I love his fair angels.

Translated from the Russian by Elaine Feinstein

PAUL VERLAINE

FRANCE • 1844–1896

The very first poem I remember is one that I read when I was fourteen. I fell in love with its melodic sound and felt profound connection to it, full of malaise and sorrow. The music of this poem has stayed with me ever since even though I have never read it again.

—Alexandra Sinclair, Beverly Hills, California

Like city's rain, my heart

The rain falls gently on the town.—ARTHUR RIMBAUD

Like city's rain, my heart
Rains teardrops too. What now,
This languorous ache, this smart
That pierces, wounds my heart?

Gentle, the sound of rain
Pattering roof and ground!
Ah, for the heart in pain,
Sweet is the sound of rain!

Tears rain—but who knows why?—
And fill my heartsick heart.
No faithless lover's lie? . . .
It mourns, and who knows why?

And nothing pains me so—
With neither love nor hate—
As simply not to know
Why my heart suffers so.

Translated from the French by Norman R. Shapiro

DEREK WALCOTT

ST. LUCIA, WEST INDIES • B. 1930

No matter how many times I reread "Streams," my scalp never fails to prickle when I read the first five lines, and much as I try to slow down and savor it, I find myself rushing through it, carried by the streams of beautiful language, to get the word "Taliesin" at the end of each stanza. It's a poem about language—the beauty of the Welsh language and of Walcott's island tongue, his mother tongue—and the connections between them. It's also about the connections between the harsh treatment of workers in Wales and the workers in the Caribbean. For me, it's also about connections between Walcott, of African and European descent, and me, of Anglo-Saxon/Welsh descent—connections made through love of language, of poetry.

—Priscilla Oppenheimer, 66, Retired Editor, Lancaster, Pennsylvania

Streams

Whenever the sunlit rain
has trawled its trickling meshes
on the dark hills back of the brain,
I keep hearing a Wales
so windswept it refreshes.
Pastures brighten with news
from drizzle-prodded sheep,
and Wales, all its green length,
from wet slate to castle keep,
and the slag hills' runnelling noise
climbs with my mother's voice
in her widowed, timbered strength,
as the pubs turn into pews
and the ale-tongued firelight dies
in talking of Taliesin.

Streams flashed there like buckles,
rooted handshakes of wrists
with corduroy voices would close
on mine, and I heard a language
built of wet stones and mists
in each stubborn bilingual sign,

in the cloud-lit country of Vaughan;
I heard under slag hills the rage
of coal-black abolitionists,
while in the tattered dress
of a lace-torn stream in the sun
the heather-haired princess
bowed with her milk-white stallion
into the embroidered leaves in
the language of Taliesin.

But I saw Wales's capital sin,
I saw Rhondda afflicted with
mineral silence, and a seine
trawl empty Aberystwyth.
Between stricken chimney stacks
on smokeless Sabbaths, starlings
drifted in cinders, curraghs
slept face down on sand, no hymn
rose from the dark throats of the mines
and if, above them, was a lark's
song, it was the only engine
with power "To Be a Pilgrim'
over paradisal miles in
the country of Taliesin.

I recognized the colonial condition.
In the green coaling station
of our harbour, there were mornes
of anthracite coal, while we prayed
in hard pews, and heard sermons
as empty as wharves, and saw the frayed
knots of miners with minstrel faces
on the wet cobbles, with their patient
caps bared at the evening Mission;
if song is the first submission,
I was humming inside the phrases
of my childhood's faith as I went
in the wake of the rain-lit sun
to the lambs and wet hills of Wales in
the harp-grass of Taliesin.

Derek Walcott

Margaret Walker

UNITED STATES · 1915–1998

I was born in an era of tremendous change in this country, the beginning of the Civil Rights Movement. I was too young to participate actively in it but I was stamped by it. It molded me, and my career was going to be devoted to doing things just, moral, and right "for my people." The definition of "my people" as I had understood it as a young girl growing up has really broadened itself as I've become a more mature woman. "My people" includes all the people of the State of Georgia, it encompasses everybody living in this country, and it's even growing now, becoming more of a worldview. Nonetheless, I still have the old concerns, which embody what I thought as a young girl growing up black in the United States.

—Leah Ward Sears, 49, Supreme Court Justice, Atlanta, Georgia

For My People

DVD, Track 28

For my people everywhere singing their slave songs repeatedly:
their dirges and their ditties and their blues and jubilees,
praying their prayers nightly to an unknown god, bending
their knees humbly to an unseen power;

For my people lending their strength to the years, to the gone
years and the now years and the maybe years, washing iron-
ing cooking scrubbing sewing mending hoeing plowing dig-
ging planting pruning patching dragging along never gaining
never reaping never knowing and never understanding.

For my playmates in the clay and dust and sand of Alabama
backyards playing baptizing and preaching and doctor and
jail and soldier and school and mama and cooking and play-
house and concert and store and hair and Miss Choomby
and company;

For the cramped bewildered years we went to school to learn to
know the reasons why and the answers to and the people
who and the places where and the days when, in memory of
the bitter hours when we discovered we were black and poor
and small and different and nobody cared and nobody won-
dered and nobody understood;

250

Margaret Walker

For the boys and girls who grew in spite of these things to be
Man and Woman, to laugh and dance and sing and play and
drink their wine and religion and success, to marry their
playmates and bear children and then die of consumption
and anemia and lynching;

For my people thronging 47th Street in Chicago and Lenox
Avenue in New York and Rampart Street in New Orleans,
lost disinherited dispossessed and happy people filling the
cabarets and taverns and other people's pockets needing
bread and shoes and milk and land and money and some-
thing—something all our own;

For my people walking blindly spreading joy, losing time being
lazy, sleeping when hungry, shouting when burdened, drink-
ing when hopeless, tied and shackled and tangled among
ourselves by the unseen creatures who tower over us omni-
sciently and laugh;

For my people blundering and groping and floundering in the
dark of churches and schools and clubs and societies, associa-
tions and councils and committees and conventions, dis-
tressed and disturbed and deceived and devoured by
money-hungry glory-craving leeches, preyed on by facile
force of state and fad and novelty, by false prophet and holy
believer;

For my people standing staring trying to fashion a better way
from confusion, from hypocrisy and misunderstanding, try-
ing to fashion a world that will hold all the people, all the
faces, all the adams and eves and their countless generations;

Let a new earth rise. Let another world be born. Let a bloody
peace be written in the sky. Let a second generation full of
courage issue forth; let a people loving freedom come to
growth. Let a beauty full of healing and a strength of final
clenching be the pulsing in our spirits and our blood. Let the
martial songs be written, let the dirges disappear. Let a race
of men now rise and take control.

I had just completed my first year of law school when my paternal grand-mother died. She was the center of my large Italian family's universe and, in many respects, my childhood passed when she did. Soon after her death I attended a benefit for our school's new Journal of Gender and the Law *at which Margaret Walker gave a reading of a number of her poems. Among her readings was "Lineage." As I listened to her speak, to her strong mea-sured tones, I was overwhelmed not only with the memories of my grand-mother and of the stories I had heard of my maternal grandmother, who died when I was a boy, but also with a sense of who I was and where I came from. I was simply amazed at how deeply the words of this seventy-year-old African American woman from the Washington, D.C., area affected me—a twenty six-year-old Italian American law student from Boston.*

—John Tocci, 35, Attorney, Dedham, Massachusetts

Lineage

My grandmothers were strong.
They followed plows and bent to toil.
They moved through fields sowing seed.
They touched earth and grain grew.
They were full of sturdiness and singing.
My grandmothers were strong.

My grandmothers are full of memories
Smelling of soap and onions and wet clay
With veins rolling roughly over quick hands
They have many clean words to say.
My grandmothers were strong.
Why am I not as they?

Edmund Waller

ENGLAND · 1606–1687

When I was eighteen, I was learning the nursing profession during World War II, and we saw firsthand the challenges of medical care. Nurses were often reminded to think of the profession as "a calling"—working overtime without a future of great financial reward. I had purchased my freshman year a paperback collection of great lyrical English and American poetry. (It's still at my bedside sixty years later.) To find Edmund Waller's "Go, Lovely Rose!" was a wonderful romantic relief. To dream of being sent forth to bloom! Was there a future when all the world seemed turned upside down?

—Elaine Ellison, 75, Retired Nurse, Minot, North Dakota

Go, Lovely Rose!

Go, lovely Rose!
Tell her that wastes her time and me
That now she knows,
When I resemble her to thee,
How sweet and fair she seems to be.

Tell her that's young,
And shuns to have her graces spied,
That hadst thou sprung
In deserts, where no men abide,
Thou must have uncommended died.

Small is the worth
Of beauty from the light retired;
Bid her come forth,
Suffer herself to be desired,
And not blush so to be admired.

Then die! that she
The common fate of all things rare
May read in thee;
How small a part of time they share
That are so wondrous sweet and fair!

Robert Penn Warren

UNITED STATES • 1905–1989

The geese, stars, and elderberry blooms in Robert Penn Warren's poem appeal to my love of natural history and to memories of my Southern childhood.
—Sandra Fisher, 50, Natural History Teacher, Arlington, Massachusetts

Tell Me a Story

A

Long ago, in Kentucky, I, a boy, stood
By a dirt road, in first dark, and heard
The great geese hoot northward.

I could not see them, there being no moon
And the stars sparse. I heard them.

I did not know what was happening in my heart.

It was the season before the elderberry blooms,
Therefore they were going north.

The sound was passing northward.

B

Tell me a story.

In this century, and moment, of mania,
Tell me a story.

Make it a story of great distances, and starlight.

The name of the story will be Time,
But you must not pronounce its name.

Tell me a story of deep delight.

WALT WHITMAN

UNITED STATES · 1819–1892

I am a lifelong college and university teacher and performer in the field of music. The first time I read this poem was in the great antiwar choral cantata, Dona Nobis Pacem *by Ralph Vaughan Williams. I was preparing choir and orchestra for a performance of this brilliant composition in the early 1970s during the Vietnam War, and was moved, as were the singers, by several strong themes: the deaths of son and father in the same battle, the image of the moon being the wife/mother figure bathing them with eternal light as they passed to burial, the tender love that Whitman showers on all these figures, and finally a sense of coming to grips with the effects of war and killing, and the hope that greater love for one another might eventually bring peace and reconciliation to humanity. The beauty of this poem so moved me that I put it on a second program entitled* Songs of Peace and War *a few years later, just as the Vietnam conflict was coming to an end. I remember well the total, respectful silence (instead of applause) in the darkened hall after our last piece.*

—Robert Rockabrand, 67, Emeritus Professor of Music, Elsah, Illinois

Dirge for Two Veterans

The last sunbeam
Lightly falls from the finish'd Sabbath,
On the pavement here—and there beyond, it is looking,
Down a new-made double grave.

Lo! the moon ascending!
Up from the east, the silvery round moon;
Beautiful over the house-tops, ghastly, phantom moon;
Immense and silent moon.

I see a sad procession,
And I hear the sound of coming full-key'd bugles;
All the channels of the city streets they're flooding,
As with voices and with tears.

I hear the great drum pounding,
And the small drums steady whirring;

And every blow of the great convulsive drums,
  Strikes me through and through.

    For the son is brought with the father
(In the foremost ranks of the fierce assault they fell;
Two veterans, son and father, dropt together,
    And the double grave awaits them).

    Now nearer blow the bugles,
And the drums strike more convulsive;
And the day-light o'er the pavement quite has faded,
    And the strong dead-march enwraps me.

    In the eastern sky up-buoying,
The sorrowful vast phantom moves illumin'd
('Tis some mother's large, transparent face,
    In heaven brighter growing).

    O strong dead-march, you please me!
O moon immense, with your silvery face you soothe me!
O my soldiers twain! O my veterans, passing to burial!
    What I have I also give you.

    The moon gives you light,
And the bugles and the drums give you music;
And my heart, O my soldiers, my veterans,
    My heart gives you love.

My son is a runner.

—Kathleen Bacich, 66, Homemaker, Brookfield, Connecticut

The Runner

On a flat road runs the well-train'd runner;
He is lean and sinewy, with muscular legs;
He is thinly clothed—he leans forward as he runs,
With lightly closed fists, and arms partially rais'd.

Walt Whitman

Song of Myself *is a poem that I probably had a lot of difficulty under-standing the first time. There were certain lines that caught me and that I liked, and when I got to the very end of this very long poem—the last half-dozen lines are so encouraging. In those last few lines Whitman tells you what you're thinking. He says, "You probably don't understand what you just read but stay with it and you will and you'll love it." That felt like it was speaking directly to me when I first read it, and I keep those lines in mind no matter what I read now.*

—John Doherty, 34, Construction Worker, Braintree, Massachusetts

from *Song of Myself* DVD, Track 2

50

There is that in me—I do not know what it is—but I know it is
   in me.

Wrench'd and sweaty—calm and cool then my body becomes,
I sleep—I sleep long.

I do not know it—it is without name—it is a word unsaid,
It is not in any dictionary, utterance, symbol.

Something it swings on more than the earth I swing on,
To it the creation is the friend whose embracing awakes me.

Perhaps I might tell more. Outlines! I plead for my brothers and
   sisters.

Do you see O my brothers and sisters?
It is not chaos or death—it is form, union, plan—it is eternal
   life—it is happiness.

52

The spotted hawk swoops by and accuses me, he complains of my
   gab and my loitering.

I too am not a bit tamed, I too am untranslatable,
I sound my barbaric yawp over the roofs of the world.

Walt Whitman

The last scud of day holds back for me,
It flings my likeness after the rest and true as any on the shadow'd
 wilds,
It coaxes me to the vapor and the dusk.

I depart as air, I shake my white locks at the runaway sun,
I effuse my flesh in eddies, and drift it in lacy jags.

I bequeath myself to the dirt to grow from the grass I love,
If you want me again look for me under your boot-soles.

You will hardly know who I am or what I mean,
But I shall be good health to you nevertheless,
And filter and fibre your blood.

Failing to fetch me at first keep encouraged,
Missing me one place search another,
I stop somewhere waiting for you.

*A year that chanted corporate reduction, my daughter's clinical depression,
my father's death and mother's terminal cancer, my wife's crushing health
concerns, the babblings of artistic despair, a search for personal value and
meaning, a year that swirled within me as I crushed my footfall to the
books in my garage, opened the first page, and rising before my anger heard
the sustaining shout of this poem!*
—Harley Palmer, 47, Visa Processing Specialist, Newmarket,
 New Hampshire

Year That Trembled and Reel'd Beneath Me

Year that trembled and reel'd beneath me!
Your summer wind was warm enough—yet the air I breathed
 froze me;
A thick gloom fell through the sunshine and darken'd me;
Must I change my triumphant songs? said I to myself;
Must I indeed learn to chant the cold dirges of the baffled?
And sullen hymns of defeat?

Walt Whitman

RICHARD WILBUR

UNITED STATES · B. 1921

Richard Wilbur captures the sensations of both runner and spectator in this poem about Boston Marathon runners as they pass along Heartbreak Hill. You feel the runners pass by in this poem, and that motion stays with you after reading it. My memories of having this feeling while participating in the Boston Marathon kept me going throughout my ordeal with breast cancer. For the 100th Boston Marathon—just one year after my surgery and chemotherapy—my husband and I ran together as we always had in earlier years. My legs retain the sensation of "driving" up that terrible mile of the race; I can feel my face clenched and runners struggling onward with me. The witnesses to this trial stand along the sidelines. They are as important to me as any cup of water I may drink.
—Ival Stratford-Kovner, 48, Painter, Dedham, Massachusetts

Patriots' Day

(Wellesley, Massachusetts)

Restless that noble day, appeased by soft
Drinks and tobacco, littering the grass
While the flag snapped and brightened far aloft,
We waited for the marathon to pass,

We fathers and our little sons, let out
Of school and office to be put to shame.
Now from the street-side someone raised a shout,
And into view the first small runners came.

Dark in the glare, they seemed to thresh in place
Like preening flies upon a window-sill,
Yet gained and grew, and at a cruel pace
Swept by us on their way to Heartbreak Hill—

Legs driving, fists at port, clenched faces, men,
And in amongst them, stamping on the sun,
Our champion Kelley, who would win again,
Rocked in his will, at rest within his run.

OSCAR WILDE

IRELAND • 1854–1900

The Harlot's House

We caught the tread of dancing feet,
We loitered down the moonlit street,
And stopped beneath the Harlot's House.
Inside, above the din and fray,
We heard the loud musicians play
The *Treues Liebes Herz* of Strauss.

Like strange mechanical grotesques,
Making fantastic arabesques,
The shadows raced across the blind.
We watched the ghostly dancers spin,
To sound of horn and violin,
Like black leaves wheeling in the wind.

Like wire-pulled Automatons,
Slim silhouetted skeletons
Went sidling through the slow quadrille,
Then took each other by the hand,
And danced a stately saraband;
Their laughter echoed thin and shrill.

Sometimes a clock-work puppet pressed
A phantom lover to her breast,
Sometimes they seemed to try and sing.
Sometimes a horrible Marionette
Came out and smoked its cigarette
Upon the steps like a live thing.

Then turning to my love I said,
"The dead are dancing with the dead,
The dust is whirling with the dust."

But she, she heard the violin,
And left my side and entered in:
Love passed into the House of Lust.

Then suddenly the tune went false,
The dancers wearied of the waltz,
The shadows ceased to wheel and whirl,
And down the long and silent street,
The dawn with silver-sandalled feet,
Crept like a frightened girl.

WILLIAM CARLOS WILLIAMS

UNITED STATES · 1883–1963

I fell in love with this poem when I was too young to appreciate it (and maybe I still am)—but the idea that we cannot live and stay free of thorns rang true for me and still does.
—Madelyn Boudreaux, 28, Computer Developer, Salt Lake City, Utah

Talk about a love poem for all ages, for the ages!
—Allan Ruter, 45, Teacher, Glenview, Illinois

The Ivy Crown

The whole process is a lie,
      unless,
            crowned by excess,
it break forcefully,
      one way or another,
            from its confinement—
or find a deeper well.
      Antony and Cleopatra
            were right;
they have shown
      the way. I love you
            or I do not live
at all.

Daffodil time
      is past. This is
            summer, summer!
the heart says,
      and not even the full of it.
            No doubts
are permitted—
      though they will come
            and may
before our time
      overwhelm us.
            We are only mortal

but being mortal
                can defy our fate.
                                We may
by an outside chance
                even win! We do not
                                look to see
jonquils and violets
                come again
                                but there are,
still,
                the roses!

Romance has no part in it.
                The business of love is
                                cruelty *which,*
by our wills,
                we transform
                                to live together.
It has its seasons,
                for and against,
                                whatever the heart
fumbles in the dark
                to assert
                                toward the end of May.
Just as the nature of briars
                is to tear flesh,
                                I have proceeded
through them.
                Keep
                                the briars out,
they say.
                You cannot live
                                and keep free of
briars.

Children pick flowers.
                Let them.
                                Though having them
in hand
                they have no further use for them

                    but leave them crumpled
at the curb's edge.

At our age the imagination
          across the sorry facts
                    lifts us
to make roses
          stand before thorns.
                    Sure
love is cruel
          and selfish
                    and totally obtuse—
at least, blinded by the light,
          young love is.
                    But we are older,
I to love
          and you to be loved,
                    we have,
no matter how,
          by our wills survived
                    to keep
the jeweled prize
          always
                    at our finger tips.
We will it so
          and so it is
                    past all accident.

Rain

As the rain falls
so does
        your love

bathe every
        open
object of the world—

In houses
the priceless dry
        rooms
of illicit love
where we live
hear the wash of the
        rain—

There
        paintings
and fine
        metalware
woven stuffs—
all the whorishness
of our
        delight
sees
from its window

the spring wash
of your love
        the falling
rain—

William Carlos Williams

The trees
are become
beasts fresh-risen
from the sea—
water

trickles
from the crevices of
their hides—

So my life is spent
    to keep out love
with which
she rains upon

   the world

of spring

   drips

so spreads

   the words

far apart to let in

    her love

And running in between

the drops

   the rain

is a kind physician

    the rain
of her thoughts over

the ocean
   every

where

William Carlos Williams

                walking with
invisible swift feet
over
        the helpless
                        waves—

Unworldly love
that has no hope
                        of the world

                        and that
cannot change the world
to its delight—

        The rain
falls upon the earth
and grass and flowers

come
        perfectly

into form from its
                        liquid

clearness

                But love is
unworldly

                and nothing
comes of it but love

following
and falling endlessly
from
        her thoughts

WILLIAM WORDSWORTH

ENGLAND • 1770–1850

*When I was eight years old, my brother—who was eleven at the time—
died in a sledding accident. That made a big difference for me, as he was a
true "big brother" who cared about and watched out for me. So, the little
eight-year-old child who spoke of her brother's death in the wintertime
insisting he was still with her was very touching, and made my brother
seem closer.*

—Kathleen Meyerdierks, 55, Teacher, Brookfield, Massachusetts

We Are Seven

————A simple Child,
That lightly draws its breath,
And feels its life in every limb,
What should it know of death?

I met a little cottage Girl:
She was eight years old, she said;
Her hair was thick with many a curl
That clustered round her head.

She had a rustic, woodland air,
And she was wildly clad:
Her eyes were fair, and very fair;
—Her beauty made me glad.

"Sisters and brothers, little Maid,
How many may you be?"
"How many? Seven in all," she said,
And wondering looked at me.

"And where are they? I pray you tell."
She answered, "Seven are we;
And two of us at Conway dwell,
And two are gone to sea.

"Two of us in the church-yard lie,
My sister and my brother;

And, in the church-yard cottage, I
Dwell near them with my mother."

"You say that two at Conway dwell,
And two are gone to sea,
Yet ye are seven! I pray you tell,
Sweet Maid, how this may be."

Then did the little Maid reply,
"Seven boys and girls are we;
Two of us in the church-yard lie,
Beneath the church-yard tree."

"You run about, my little Maid,
Your limbs they are alive;
If two are in the church-yard laid,
Then ye are only five."

"Their graves are green, they may be seen,"
The little Maid replied,
"Twelve steps or more from my mother's door,
And they are side by side.

"My stockings there I often knit,
My kerchief there I hem;
And there upon the ground I sit,
And sing a song to them.

"And often after sun-set, Sir,
When it is light and fair,
I take my little porringer,
And eat my supper there.

"The first that died was sister Jane;
In bed she moaning lay,
Till God released her of her pain;
And then she went away.

"So in the church-yard she was laid;
And, when the grass was dry,
Together round her grave we played,
My brother John and I.

"And when the ground was white with snow,
And I could run and slide,
My brother John was forced to go,
And he lies by her side."

"How many are you, then," said I,
"If they two are in heaven?"
Quick was the little Maid's reply,
"O Master! we are seven."

"But they are dead; those two are dead!
Their spirits are in heaven!"
'Twas throwing words away; for still
The little Maid would have her will,
And said, "Nay, we are seven!"

The world is too much with us; late and soon

The world is too much with us; late and soon,
Getting and spending, we lay waste our powers:
Little we see in Nature that is ours;
We have given our hearts away, a sordid boon!
This Sea that bares her bosom to the moon;
The winds that will be howling at all hours,
And are up-gathered now like sleeping flowers;
For this, for everything, we are out of tune;
It moves us not.—Great God! I'd rather be
A Pagan suckled in a creed outworn;
So might I, standing on this pleasant lea,
Have glimpses that would make me less forlorn;
Have sight of Proteus rising from the sea;
Or hear old Triton blow his wreathèd horn.

CHARLES WRIGHT

UNITED STATES • B. 1935

This poem gives me the sense of what my father is going through and what he is feeling at this age. My father is a man in his late forties and I think that he is going through a midlife crisis because he walks around the house with nothing to do. He's upset with everything and he just goes on the back porch and stands there alone, probably thinking about what he has done in life and what he hasn't done. I think my brother and I don't help him with this situation; I think we could do more things with him so he'd forget he has worries and problems. The poet describes himself as a mockingbird; I think my father could relate to that because a mockingbird is a bird that flies around copying other birds' songs because it doesn't know what to do. The poet makes me feel that he has nothing to live for; sometimes I think my dad feels the same way, but then he sees that he has children that care about him even though they don't show it very often. He also has a wife who loves him, a family that loves him very dearly.

—Z. V., 15, Student, Brooklyn, New York

After Reading Tu Fu, I Go Outside to the Dwarf Orchard

East of me, west of me, full summer.
How deeper than elsewhere the dusk is in your own yard.
Birds fly back and forth across the lawn

                    looking for home

As night drifts up like a little boat.

Day after day, I become of less use to myself.
Like this mockingbird,
                  I flit from one thing to the next.
What do I have to look forward to at fifty-four?
Tomorrow is dark.
               Day-after-tomorrow is darker still.

The sky dogs are whimpering.
Fireflies are dragging the hush of evening
                  up from the damp grass.

Into the world's tumult, into the chaos of every day,
Go quietly, quietly.

JAMES WRIGHT

UNITED STATES · 1927–1980

The poem is set in Minnesota. I grew up in the state next door to Minnesota and have experienced the same sort of feeling Wright is talking about here. It's the mystery of the last line that intrigues me. Also, I love the cowbells following one another because, of course, it's the cows that follow, not the bells.
—Carol O'Toole, 73, Retired, San Francisco, California

It's beautiful and heart-wrenching at the same time, as if the summation of an entire life were contained in thirteen lines.
—Jerry Peck, 63, Computer Analyst, Iowa City, Iowa

As a young man trying to figure out which path to take, I feel this poem captures the most significant fear I have.
—Robert Ahera, 24, Entomologist, Laramie, Wyoming

Lying in a Hammock at William Duffy's Farm in Pine Island, Minnesota

Over my head, I see the bronze butterfly,
Asleep on the black trunk,
Blowing like a leaf in green shadow.
Down the ravine behind the empty house,
The cowbells follow one another
Into the distances of the afternoon.
To my right,
In a field of sunlight between two pines,
The droppings of last year's horses
Blaze up into golden stones.
I lean back, as the evening darkens and comes on.
A chicken hawk floats over, looking for home.
I have wasted my life.

THOMAS WYATT

ENGLAND • 1503–1542

Other poems are just amazing, beautiful, artistic word games compared to true poems. This is a true poem.
—Rachel Castignoli, 20, Student, Chicago, Illinois

Whoso List To Hunt

Whoso list to hunt, I know where is an hind,
But as for me, alas, I may no more;
The vain travail hath wearied me so sore,
I am of them that furthest come behind.
Yet may I by no means my wearied mind
Draw from the deer, but as she fleeth afore
Fainting I follow; I leave off therefore,
Since in a net I seek to hold the wind.
Who list her hunt, I put him out of doubt,
As well as I, may spend his time in vain.
And graven with diamonds in letters plain,
There is written her fair neck round about,
"*Noli me tangere,* for Caesar's I am,
And wild for to hold, though I seem tame."

WILLIAM BUTLER YEATS

IRELAND · 1865–1939

I was a daddy's girl. In our family scrapbook, there is a picture of me at about three. Below it, my father had pasted this poem. That page still means the world to me even though my father has been gone now for thirty-five years and I am coming up on my seventieth birthday.

—Pat Becker, 68, Retired Medical Transcriber, Phoenix, Arizona

A Prayer for My Daughter

Once more the storm is howling, and half hid
Under this cradle-hood and coverlid
My child sleeps on. There is no obstacle
But Gregory's wood and one bare hill
Whereby the haystack- and roof-levelling wind,
Bred on the Atlantic, can be stayed;
And for an hour I have walked and prayed
Because of the great gloom that is in my mind.

I have walked and prayed for this young child an hour
And heard the sea-wind scream upon the tower,
And under the arches of the bridge, and scream
In the elms above the flooded stream;
Imagining in excited reverie
That the future years had come,
Dancing to a frenzied drum,
Out of the murderous innocence of the sea.

May she be granted beauty and yet not
Beauty to make a stranger's eye distraught,
Or hers before a looking-glass, for such,
Being made beautiful overmuch,
Consider beauty a sufficient end,
Lose natural kindness and maybe
The heart-revealing intimacy
That chooses right, and never find a friend.

Helen being chosen found life flat and dull
And later had much trouble from a fool,

While that great Queen, that rose out of the spray,
Being fatherless could have her way
Yet chose a bandy-leggèd smith for man.
It's certain that fine women eat
A crazy salad with their meat
Whereby the Horn of Plenty is undone.

In courtesy I'd have her chiefly learned;
Hearts are not had as a gift but hearts are earned
By those that are not entirely beautiful;
Yet many, that have played the fool
For beauty's very self, has charm made wise,
And many a poor man that has roved,
Loved and thought himself beloved,
From a glad kindness cannot take his eyes.

May she become a flourishing hidden tree
That all her thoughts may like the linnet be,
And have no business but dispensing round
Their magnanimities of sound,
Nor but in merriment begin a chase,
Nor but in merriment a quarrel.
O may she live like some green laurel
Rooted in one dear perpetual place.

My mind, because the minds that I have loved,
The sort of beauty that I have approved,
Prosper but little, has dried up of late,
Yet knows that to be choked with hate
May well be of all evil chances chief.
If there's no hatred in a mind
Assault and battery of the wind
Can never tear the linnet from the leaf.

An intellectual hatred is the worst,
So let her think opinions are accursed.
Have I not seen the loveliest woman born
Out of the mouth of Plenty's horn,
Because of her opinionated mind
Barter that horn and every good

By quiet natures understood
For an old bellows full of angry wind?

Considering that, all hatred driven hence,
The soul recovers radical innocence
And learns at last that it is self-delighting,
Self-appeasing, self-affrighting,
And that its own sweet will is Heaven's will;
She can, though every face should scowl
And every windy quarter howl
Or every bellows burst, be happy still.

And may her bridegroom bring her to a house
Where all's accustomed, ceremonious;
For arrogance and hatred are the wares
Peddled in the thoroughfares.
How but in custom and in ceremony
Are innocence and beauty born?
Ceremony's a name for the rich horn,
And custom for the spreading laurel tree.

When my father died at the age of eighty a few years ago, my sister and I went on the sad trip to Tenerife in the Canary Islands, his final home. Arranging for a cremation was a job in and of itself in Spanish Tenerife, and then we needed to think of the right thing to say that might somehow touch on our dad's spirit. A friend in Tenerife helped us find this Yeats poem, which we recognized immediately as reflecting his insatiable thirst for knowledge. Now Yeats's words are becoming more and more personal, and I hope for foolish passion, and, if I'm lucky, wisdom.

—Kerry Cooke, 52, Medical Writer, Boise, Idaho

A Prayer for Old Age

God guard me from those thoughts men think
In the mind alone;
He that sings a lasting song
Thinks in a marrow-bone;

From all that makes a wise old man
That can be praised of all;
O what am I that I should not seem
For the song's sake a fool?

I pray—for fashion's word is out
And prayer comes round again—
That I may seem, though I die old,
A foolish, passionate man.

When Yeats wrote "Politics," it was his final opinion on the whole matter
of the comparison of politics versus love, and a person like William Butler
Yeats chose love. I respect that very much because he considered that his
parting shot. I can see where he's right. I think that's going to be my parting
shot, too.
—Steve Conteagüero, 28, United States Marine, Miami, Florida

Politics   *DVD, Track 4*

"In our time the destiny of man presents its meaning
in political terms."—THOMAS MANN

How can I, that girl standing there,
My attention fix
On Roman or on Russian
Or on Spanish politics?
Yet here's a travelled man that knows
What he talks about,
And there's a politician
That has read and thought,
And maybe what they say is true
Of war and war's alarms,
But O that I were young again
And held her in my arms!

Sone no Yoshitada

JAPAN · LATE TENTH CENTURY

I love watching the sunset on the beach. We live right next to the beach and I can just walk out there some nights and watch it. Or we'll be driving and I'll look out the window and there's always purple or orange or some wonderful combination of colors that sets me in awe.

—Kiyoshi Houston, 14, Student, Santa Monica, California

The lower leaves of the trees

DVD, Track 10

The lower leaves of the trees
Tangle the sunset in dusk.
Awe spreads with
The summer twilight.

Translated from the Japanese by Kenneth Rexroth

SAADI YOUSSEF

IRAQ • B. 1934

I was looking through poetry books when I stumbled onto this poem. It brought up what happens in school, home, and just plain life. When I come home, sometimes upset from being picked on, my mother says what this poem says but in different words. At night I feel the same way, so when I came upon a poem called "Attention" it caught my attention!
—Shala M., 12, Student, Falmouth, Massachusetts

Attention

Those who come by me passing,
I will remember them,
and those who come heavy and overbearing,
I will forget.
. . . .
. . . .
. . . .
This is why
when air gushes between mountains
we describe the wind
and forget the rocks.

Translated from the Arabic by Khaled Mattawa

ZAWGEE
BURMA • 1907–1990

I think poetry has played an important part in the lives of people in Burma, perhaps only by default, because there wasn't much television—there was no television, at least when we were growing up—so we spent a lot of time with books and reading. . . . I've known this poem since my childhood. . . . Zawgee was using a fairly commonly found object in nature as a symbol of life in Burma. And he was trying to—that's what it says to me—paint a picture of overcoming obstacles.

—Lyn Aye, 52, Anesthesiologist, Auburn, California

The Way of the Water-Hyacinth   DVD, *Track 27*

Bobbing on the breeze blown waves
Bowing to the tide
Hyacinth rises and falls

Falling but not felled
By flotsam, twigs, leaves
She ducks, bobs and weaves.

Ducks, ducks by the score
Jolting, quacking and more
She spins through—

Spinning, swamped, slimed, sunk
She rises, resolute
Still crowned by petals.

Translated from the Burmese by Lyn Aye

Notes

Jonson, Ben, "Inviting a Friend to Supper." Throughout this book, we editors have modernized archaic spelling, except in cases where we think the meter, meaning or an author's personal elements of style would be affected. Here, the seventeenth-century spellings have been preserved to reflect the contributor's mention of them in his letter.

Pessoa, Fernando. The poem ("When in the widening circle of rebirth") is the twentieth in Pessoa's sequence *35 Sonnets,* and was written originally in English, though the poet wrote more often in his native language, Portuguese.

Warren, Robert Penn. "Tell Me a Story" is the seventh and final poem in the sequence titled *Audubon: A Vision.*

Wilbur, Richard. "Patriots' Day" is the second of three parts of the poem "Running."

Permissions

Anna Akhmatova, "The Sentence," translated by Judith Hemschemeyer, from *Complete Poems of Anna Akhmatova, Updated and Expanded Edition,* edited by Roberta Reeder. Copyright © 1989, 1992, 1997 by Judith Hemschemeyer. Reprinted with the permission of Zephyr Press.

Dante Alighieri, "The Great Canzon," translated by Kenneth Rexroth, from *The Collected Shorter Poems of Kenneth Rexroth.* Copyright © 1966 by Kenneth Rexroth. Reprinted with the permission of New Directions Publishing Corporation.

Yehuda Amichai, "Inside the Apple," translated by Chana Bloch, from *Selected Poetry of Yehuda Amichai,* edited by Chana Bloch and Stephen Mitchell. Copyright © 1986, 1996 by Chana Bloch and Stephen Mitchell. Reprinted with the permission of the University of California Press.

A. R. Ammons, "In Memoriam Mae Noblitt" from *A Coast of Trees.* Copyright © 1981 by A.R. Ammons. Reprinted with the permission of W. W. Norton & Company, Inc.

John Ashbery, "A Blessing in Disguise" from *Rivers and Mountains.* Copyright © 1962, 1963, 1964, 1966 by John Ashbery. Reprinted with the permission of Georges Borchardt, Inc., for the author. "This Room" from *Your Name Here.* Copyright © 2000 by John Ashbery. Reprinted with the permission of Farrar, Straus & Giroux, LLC.

Margaret Atwood, "It Is Dangerous to Read Newspapers" from *Selected Poems 1965–1975.* Copyright © 1976 by Margaret Atwood. Reprinted with the permission of Houghton Mifflin Company and Oxford University Press Canada. All rights reserved.

288

291

294

Index

Absence of Joaquín 176
"A cold coming we had of it 72
A cold spring: 28
After Apple-Picking 75
After Reading Tu Fu, I Go Outside to the Dwarf Orchard 272
Afterwards 93
Again last night I dreamed the dream called Laundry 164
A hundred mountains and no bird 151
Aiken, Conrad 3
Akhmatova, Anna 4
Alighieri, Dante 5
All others talked as if 144
All out-of-doors looked darkly in at him 78
Alone 191
A long time ago, when I was a child 175
Although it is a cold evening 25
A man and a woman are sitting at a table 74
Amanda, you'll be going 136
A May morning 34
Amichai, Yehuda 7
Ammons, A. R. 8

Ample make this Bed— (829) 58
And so for nights 97
And the stone word fell 4
And tomorrow morning at 8 o'clock in Springfield, Massachusetts 180
—And when you have forgotten the bright bedclothes on a Wednesday and a Saturday 37
A poem should be palpable and mute 162
Ars Poetica 162
Arundel Tomb, An 141
As an unperfect actor on the stage (*Sonnets* 23) 214
A serious moment for the water is when it boils 129
Ashbery, John 10
—A simple Child 268
As the rain falls 265
A thing of beauty is a joy for ever: 125
Attention 280
At the Fishhouses 25
At the New Year 185
Atwood, Margaret 12

Auden, W. H. 14
Ay, Ay, Ay de la Grifa Negra 43
Ay, ay, ay that am kinky-haired
and pure black 43

Back out of all this now too
much for us 76
Baudelaire, Charles 17
Because my mouth 111
Beckett, Samuel 19
Bent double, like old beggars
under sacks 183
Bent with worry 246
Bent with worry, God 246
Berryman, John 23
Bishop, Elizabeth 25
Black milk of daybreak we drink
it at evening 48
Blake, William 31
Blessing in Disguise, A 10
Blossom, The 34
Bobbing on the breeze blown
waves 281
Bogan, Louise 33
Boiling Water, The 129
Boland, Eavan 34
Bring me all of your dreams 111
Brooks, Gwendolyn 36
Brown, Sterling A. 38
Browning, Robert 41
Burgos, Julia de 43
Burns, Robert 45

Caedmon 144
Carrion Comfort 107
Casey at the Bat 239
Celan, Paul 48
Centaur, The 231
Chimney Sweeper, The 31
Clearances 100

Cold rapid hands 186
Cold Spring, A 28
Collar, The 102
Come hither all sweet maidens,
soberly 126
Cowper, William 50
Crane, Hart 52
Crows, The 33
Cullen, Countee 54
Cummings, E. E. 56

Dark Summer 33
Dawn 186
Day Lady Died, The 178
Deathfugue 48
Degrees of Gray in Philipsburg
113
Diamond Cutters, The 193
Dickinson, Emily 58
Directive 76
Dirge for Two Veterans 255
Discordants 3
Disillusionment of Ten O'Clock
227
Donne, John 62
Dream Keeper, The 111
Drummond de Andrade,
Carlos 67
Dulce Et Decorum Est 183
Dunn, Stephen 70

East of me, west of me, full
summer 272
*Effort at Speech Between Two
People* 207
Elephant, The 67
Eleven Addresses to Our Lord
23
Eliot, T. S. 72
Endymion 125

Enueg 1 19
Enueg 2 21
Envoy of Mr Cogito 104
*Epithalamion, Or Marriage Song,
on the Lady Elizabeth and
Court Palatine Being
Married on St. Valentine's
Day, An* 62
Erat Hora 192
Evacuee, The 244
Exeo in a spasm 19
Explosion, The 143
Eye, The 118

Facing It 134
Ferry, David 74
Finding a Long Gray Hair 128
Flower-Fed Buffaloes, The 149
For a Poet 54
Forced from home, and all its
pleasures 50
Forms of Love, The 181
For My People 250
For my people everywhere
singing their slave songs
repeatedly: 250
From childhood's hour I have
not been 191
From now on, like a departure
seen from a distance 176
Frost, Robert 75

Garden of Love, The 32
Gift, The 222
Ginsberg, Allen 82
Gitanjali 236
Glück, Louise 84
God guard me from those
thoughts men think 277
God's Grandeur 108

Goethe, Johann Wolfgang von
85
Go, Lovely Rose! 253
Gone, I say and walk from
church 213
Good-Morrow, The 66
Go where those others went to
the dark boundary 104
Grass so little has to do—, The
(333) 58
Gray, Thomas 86
Great Canzon, The 5
Gunn, Thom 88

"Had he and I but met 94
Hail Bishop Valentine, whose
day this is 62
Hall, Donald 90
Halliday, Mark 91
Hardy, Thomas 93
Harlot's House, The 260
Hass, Robert 95
Hayden, Robert 97
Heaney, Seamus 100
Hecht, Anthony 101
He lived—childhood summers
177
Hellvellyn 211
Herbert, George 102
Herbert, Zbigniew 104
Herrick, Robert 106
Holy Longing, The 85
Hopkins, Gerard Manley 107
Hornworm: Autumn Lamentation
138
Housman, A. E. 110
How can anyone know that a
whale 165
How can I, that girl standing
there 278

However legendary 193
Hughes, Langston 111
Hugo, Richard 113

I am a miner. The light burns
    blue 189
i carry your heart with me . . .
    56
i carry your heart with me(i carry
    it in 56
I climbed the dark brow of the
    mighty Hellvellyn 211
Idea of Trust, The 88
If I were tickled by the rub of love
    241
I have come at last to the short
    5
I have walked through many
    lives 139
I have wrapped my dreams in a
    silken cloth 54
Ikkyu 115
I Knew a Woman 204
I knew a woman, lovely in her
    bones 204
I make an elephant 67
I'm going out to clean the
    pasture spring 81
I'm Nobody! Who are you? (288)
    59
In a Dark Time 205
In a dark time, the eye begins to
    see 205
In a field 230
Initiation 197
In Memoriam A.H.H. 238
In Memoriam Mae Noblitt 8
In moving-slow he has no Peer
    206
Inside the Apple 7

In the shape of this night, in the
    still fall 185
In the small beauty of the forest
    182
Inviting a Friend to Supper 122
I play it cool 112
I scrub the long floorboards 128
Islands, The 116
Isn't it nice that everyone has a
    grocery list 91
Is There for Honest Poverty 45
I struck the board and cried,
    "No more 102
*It Is Dangerous to Read
    Newspapers* 12
It is ten years since I have seen
    these shirts 223
It is 12:20 in New York a Friday
    178
It was a beauty that I saw 123
Ivy Crown, The 262
I went to the Garden of Love 32
I wonder, by my troth, what
    thou and I 66
I wonder do you feel to-day 41

Jarrell, Randall 116
Jeffers, Robinson 118
Jellyfish, A 172
John Anderson My Jo 47
John Anderson my jo, John 47
Jones, Evan 119
Jonson, Ben 122
Journey of the Magi 72
Justice, Donald 124

Keats, John 125
Keeping Things Whole 230
Kenyon, Jane 128
Koch, Kenneth 129

Komunyakaa, Yusef 134
Kumin, Maxine 136
Kunitz, Stanley 138

Lana Turner has collapsed! 179
Language Lesson 1976 163
Larkin, Philip 141
Layers, The 139
Lay your sleeping head, my love 14
Levertov, Denise 144
Levine, Philip 146
Like city's rain, my heart 247
Lindsay, Vachel 149
Lineage 252
L'Invitation au Voyage 17
Li Po 150
Little feet of children 170
Liu Zongyuan 151
Long ago, in Kentucky, I, a boy, stood 254
Longfellow, Henry Wadsworth 152
Looking up at the stars, I know quite well 16
Lovelace, Richard 154
Lovel's Song 123
Love's Philosophy 218
Lowell, Robert 156
lower leaves of the trees, The 279
Lullaby 14
Lying in a Hammock at William Duffy's Farm in Pine Island, Minnesota 273

Machado, Antonio 160
MacLeish, Archibald 162
Mad Scene, The 164
Man He Killed, The 94

Man, if I said once, "I know" 116
Many are making love. Up above, the angels 95
McHugh, Heather 163
Meditatio 192
Meeting of the Waters, The 174
Memories of West Street and Lepke 156
Men at Forty 124
Merrill, James 164
Merwin, W. S. 165
Millay, Edna St. Vincent 166
Milosz, Czeslaw 168
Milton, John 169
Minstrel Man 111
Mistral, Gabriela 170
Moonlight in front of my bed— 150
Moore, Marianne 172
Moore, Thomas 174
More Loving One, The 16
Motto 112
Music I heard with you was more than music 3
My black face fades 134
My childhood is memories of a patio in Seville 160
My child, my sister 17
My grandmothers were strong 252
My long two-pointed ladder's sticking through a tree 75
My old flame, my wife! 158
My real dwelling 115
My whole life has led me here 90

Negro's Complaint, The 50
Nemerov, Howard 175

Neruda, Pablo 176
Never love with all your heart
    54
Nick and the Candlestick 189
Niedecker, Lorine 177
Night-Blooming Cereus, The 97
Notes from a Nonexistent
    Himalayan Expedition 234
Not, I'll not, carrion comfort,
    Despair, not feast on thee
    107

Ode on the Death of a Favorite
    Cat 86
O'Hara, Frank 178
Old Flame, The 158
Old Man's Winter Night, An 78
On a flat road runs the well-
    train'd runner 256
On a Leander Which Miss
    Reynolds, My Kind Friend,
    Gave Me 126
Once more the storm is howling,
    and half hid 275
One need not be a Chamber—to
    be Haunted— (670) 60
On Hearing a Symphony of
    Beethoven 166
Only teaching on Tuesdays,
    book-worming 156
On the day of the explosion 142
Oppen, George 181
O soft embalmer of the still
    midnight 126
Out of burlap sacks, out of
    bearing butter 146
"*Out, Out—*" 79
Oven Bird, The 81
Over my head, I see the bronze
    butterfly 273

Owen, Wilfred 183
O, yet we trust that somehow
    good 238

Parked in the fields 181
Pasture, The 81
Patchen, Kenneth 185
Patriots' Day 259
Paz, Octavio 186
Pessoa, Fernando 188
Phantasia for Elvira Shatayev
    194
Piececitos 170
Plath, Sylvia 189
Poe, Edgar Allan 191
Poem (And tomorrow morning at
    8 o'clock in Springfield,
    Massachusetts) 180
Poem (Lana Turner has col-
    lapsed!) 179
Politics 278
Population 91
Portrait 160
Pound, Ezra 192
Prayer for My Daughter, A
    275
Prayer for Old Age, A 277
Privilege of Being 95
Prospects 101
Psalm 182
Psalm of Life, A 152

Rabbit as King of the Ghosts, A
    228
Rain 265
Recuerdo 167
Requiem for the Death of a Boy
    198
Restless that noble day, appeased
    by soft 259

Rich, Adrienne 193
Rilke, Rainer Maria 197
River-Snow 151
Robinson, Edwin Arlington
    201
Roethke, Theodore 204
Rukeyser, Muriel 207
Runner, The 256

Sadness of My Neighbors, The
    237
Sappho 209
School Children, The 84
Schwartz, Delmore 210
Scott, Sir Walter 211
Seen through a Window 74
Sentence, The 4
Sexton, Anne 213
Shakespeare, William 214
Sheaves, The 201
Shelley, Percy Bysshe 218
She woke up under a loose quilt
    244
Shirt Poem, The 223
Shore, The 165
Side by side, their faces blurred
    141
Since that first morning when I
    crawled 138
Sloth, The 206
Snow Globe, The 175
Sole watchman of the flying
    stars, guard me 23
Some Dreams They Forgot 30
Somehow, one expects 237
Song in Spite of Myself 55
Song of Myself 257
Song of the Banana Man, The
    119
So these are the Himalayas 234

Speak to me. Take my hand.
    What are you now? 207
Spenser, Edmund 221
Stafford, William 222
Stanzas written in Dejection—
    December 1818, Near
    Naples 219
Stern, Gerald 223
Stevens, Wallace 227
Still Night Thoughts 150
Strand, Mark 230
Streams 248
Strong Men 38
Sunday Morning Apples 52
Surgeons must be very careful
    (108) 61
Sweet is the rose, but grows upon a
    brere 221
Sweet sounds, oh, beautiful
    music, do not cease! 166
Swenson, May 231
Szymborska, Wisława 234

Tagore, Rabindranath 236
Tate, James 237
Tell a wise person, or else keep
    silent 85
Tell Me a Story 254
Tell me not, in mournful
    numbers 152
Tennyson, Alfred, Lord 238
"Thank you, whatever comes."
    And then she turned 192
That time of year thou mayst in
    me behold (Sonnets 73)
    215
Thayer, Ernest Lawrence 239
The Atlantic is a stormy moat;
    and the Mediterranean
    118

The buzz saw snarled and rattled in the yard 79
The children go forward with their little satchels 84
The cold felt cold until our blood 194
The dead birds fell, but no one had seen them fly 30
The difficulty to think at the end of day 228
The flower-fed buffaloes of the spring 149
The flower in the glass peanut bottle formerly in the kitchen 82
The fountains mingle with the river 218
The Grass so little has to do— 58
The houses are haunted 227
The idea of trust, or 88
The last sunbeam 255
The leaves will fall again sometime and fill 52
The lower leaves of the trees 279
The outlook wasn't brilliant for the Mudville nine that day 239
There is a singer everyone has heard 81
There is not in the wide world a valley so sweet 174
There is that in me—I do not know what it is—but I know it is in me 257
The room I entered was a dream of this room 11
The saris go by me from the embassies 117
The summer that I was ten— 231
The Sun is warm, the sky is clear 219
The water hollowed the stone 186
The whole process is a lie 262
The woman who has grown old 33
The world is charged with the grandeur of God 108
The world is too much with us; late and soon 271
They dragged you from homeland 38
They Feed They Lion 146
Thinking of Death and Dogfood 136
This is just a place: 8
This Room 11
Thomas, Dylan 241
Thomas, R. S. 244
Those who come by me passing 280
Time wants to show you a different country. It's the one 222
Tired and Unhappy, You Think of Houses 210
To Althea, from Prison 154
To fight aloud, is very brave— (126) 61
To hold a damaged sparrow 71
To night, grave sir, both my poore house, and I 122
To seem the stranger lies my lot . . . 109
To seem the stranger lies my lot, my life 109
To Sleep 127

Touris, white man, wipin his face 119

Transcription of Organ Music 82

Truth the Dead Know, The 213

Tsvetaeva, Marina 246

'Twas on a lofty vase's side 86

Two in the Campagna 41

Under the thunder-dark, the cicadas resound 33

Unforgiven, The 202

Upon Julia's Clothes 106

Verlaine, Paul 247

Visible, invisible 172

Walcott, Derek 248

Walker, Margaret 250

Waller, Edmund 253

Warren, Robert Penn 254

Way of the Water-Hyacinth 281

We Are Seven 268

We caught the tread of dancing feet 260

We have set out from here for the sublime 101

We Real Cool 36

We real cool. We 36

We stand in the rain in a long line 147

We were very tired, we were very merry— 167

What Are Years? 173

What is our innocence 173

What Work Is 147

When all the others were away at Mass 100

When Americans say a man 163

When as in silks my Julia goes 106

Whenever the sunlit rain 248

When forty winters shall besiege thy brow (Sonnets 2) 217

When he, who is the unforgiven 202

When I carefully consider the curious habits of dogs 192

When I consider how my light is spent 169

When, in disgrace with Fortune and men's eyes (Sonnets 29) 216

When in the widening circle of rebirth 188

When I was one-and-twenty 110

When Love with unconfinèd wings 154

When my mother died I was very young 31

When the Present latched its postern behind my tremulous stay 93

when you have forgotten Sunday: the love story 37

Where long the shadows of the wind had rolled 201

Where the mind is without fear and the head is held high 236

While I was building neat 12

Whitman, Walt 255

Whoever you are, go out into the evening 197

Whoso List To Hunt 274

Whoso list to hunt, I know where is an hind 274

Why did I print upon myself the names 198

Wilbur, Richard 259

Wilde, Oscar 260

Williams, William Carlos 262
Wind and Water and Stone 187
With his venom 209
With No Experience in Such
Matters 71
Woman at the Washington Zoo,
The 117
Woolworth's 90
Wordsworth, William 268
world is too much with us; late
and soon, The 271
world world world world
21
Wright, Charles 272
Wright, James 273
Wyatt, Thomas 274

Year That Trembled and Reel'd
Beneath Me 258
Yeats, William Butler 275
Yes, they are alive and can have
those colours 10
Yoshitada, Sone no 279
You might come here Sunday on
a whim 113
You shall not despair 243
Youssef, Saadi 280
You visit me inside the apple 7
You Who Wronged 168
You who wronged a simple man
168

Zawgee 281

DVD Contents

Track	Page	Poem, Poet, Reader	Time
1		Introduction by Robert Pinsky	4:21
2	257	From *Song of Myself* by Walt Whitman Read by John Doherty	5:03
3	111	"Minstrel Man" by Langston Hughes Read by Pov Chin	3:53
4	278	"Politics" by William Butler Yeats Read by Steve Conteagüero	4:56
5	85	"The Holy Longing" by Johann Wolfgang von Goethe Read by Olivia Milward	3:50
6	179	"Poem" ("Lana Turner has collapsed!") by Frank O'Hara Read by Richard Samuel	2:51
7	134	"Facing It" by Yusef Komunyakaa Read by Michael H. Lythgoe	3:34
8	36	"We Real Cool" by Gwendolyn Brooks Read by John Ulrich	4:22
9	189	"Nick and the Candlestick" by Sylvia Plath Read by Seph Rodney	5:44
10	279	"The lower leaves of the trees" by Sone no Yoshitada Read by Kiyoshi Houston	2:45
11	216	"When, in disgrace with Fortune and men's eyes" by William Shakespeare Read by Daniel McCall	4:33
12	43	"Ay, Ay, Ay de la Grifa Negra" by Julia de Burgos Read by Glaisma Pérez-Silva	6:45

Track	Page	Poem, Poet, Reader	Time
13	59	"I'm Nobody! Who are you?" by Emily Dickinson Read by Yina Liang	4:59
14	79	" 'Out, Out—' " by Robert Frost Read by Elizabeth Wojtusik	6:23
15	206	"The Sloth" by Theodore Roethke Read by Katherine Mechling	3:47
16	108	"God's Grandeur" by Gerard Manley Hopkins Read by Stanley Kunitz	3:58
17	138	"Hornworm: Autumn Lamentation" by Stanley Kunitz Read by Donna Bickel	5:29
18	119	"The Song of the Banana Man" by Evan Jones Read by George Scott	7:19
19	170	"Piececitos" by Gabriela Mistral Read by Maria Christina Sanchez Escobar	4:10
20	183	"Dulce Et Decorum Est" by Wilfred Owen Read by Mary McWhorter	5:00
21	152	"A Psalm of Life" by Henry Wadsworth Longfellow Read by Michael Haynes	6:39
22	234	"Notes from a Nonexistent Himalayan Expedition" by Wisława Szymborska Read by Bill Hayes	3:30
23	236	From *Gitanjali* by Rabindranath Tagore Read by Jayashree Chatterjee	5:05
24	239	"Casey at the Bat" by Ernest Lawrence Thayer Read by Lee Samuel	5:12
25	4	"The Sentence" by Anna Akhmatova Read by Nancy Nersessian	6:07
26	25	"At the Fishhouses" by Elizabeth Bishop Read by Alexander Scherr	6:57
27	281	"The Way of the Water-Hyacinth" by Zawgee Read by Lyn Aye	5:06
28	250	"For My People" by Margaret Walker Read by Leah Ward Sears	6:31
29		Production Credits	1:56